week

A GUIDE TO UNITED KINGDOM AND EUROPEAN UNION COMPETITION POLICY

Also by Nick Gardner

DECADE OF DISCONTENT

A Guide to United Kingdom and European Union Competition Policy

Second Edition

Nick Gardner

First edition (*A Guide to United Kingdom and European
Community Competition Policy*) 1990
Second edition 1996

Published by
MACMILLAN PRESS LTD
Houndmills, Basingstoke, Hampshire RG21 6XS
and London
Companies and representatives
throughout the world

ISBN 0–333–63109–9

A catalogue record for this book is available
from the British Library.

10   9   8   7   6   5   4   3   2   1
05 04 03 02 01 00 99 98 97 96

Printed in Great Britain by
Ipswich Book Co Ltd, Ipswich, Suffolk

To my family

Contents

List of Tables

Preface

Those who are best qualified to write a book on this subject are far too busy to do so. Some of them have nevertheless been unstinting with their help and encouragement. Although I have relied throughout upon published material, the condensation which has been necessary to put it into an ordered and readable form raised serious dangers of inaccuracy, misinterpretation and false emphasis. Without help, it would have been rash for an outsider to attempt the task of providing businessmen with an insight into the inner workings of competition policy in Britain.

My heartfelt thanks go in particular to Martin Howe of the Office of Fair Trading and to Alan Blair and Noel Ing of the Monopolies and Mergers Commission for their painstaking and thought-provoking comments.

I have sought to inform rather than to criticise. The views and judgements which are nevertheless included are my own, and not those of the people who have helped me; and that, I am sure, will be true also of any errors.

NICK GARDNER

xi

Part I
The Framework of
Competition Policy

1 Ideas and their Implementation

A INTRODUCTION

This book is intended as a practical guide to the way in which competition policy works in Britain. It is written for businessmen, not for lawyers. Its summary of the legislative framework is designed for ease of reference, and the reader must look elsewhere for detailed textual analyses of the statutes. Its focus is the regulatory treatment of business conduct, most of which is determined primarily by organisational, procedural and philosophical influences rather than by matters of legal interpretation. Interpretations of the law by the Restrictive Practices Court are dealt with only to the extent needed for a broad understanding of their present impact upon business conduct: other writers have dealt comprehensively with that branch of competition law. In other respects, however, the book attempts a more comprehensive and more accessible coverage than has hitherto been available.

The reader is invited to explore the contents of this book either consecutively or selectively. A businessman who is concerned mainly with the attitudes of the regulatory authorities to a particular action which he has in mind may wish to go straight to the chapter in Part II which surveys their treatment of that type of action. If he then feels the need to understand more about the reasons for the attitudes of the authorities, or about the way in which they conduct their business, he may wish to return to some of the sections of Part I for an outline of the ideological, legislative or administrative framework within which they operate. The reader who is more concerned to get a general understanding of how the system works may prefer to start his reading here, and where necessary to skip through those sections of Parts I and II which treat particular topics in more detail than he requires. The general reader may then wish to turn to the survey in Part III of the past achievements and the possible future development of competition policy.

The legislative framework of competition policy, which is the subject of the next chapter, provides no more than a broad indication of the intentions of the policymakers who devised it. It delegates to the authorities which it appoints, a wide range of discretion in their performance of the task of giving practical effect to those intentions. That discretion is not exercised in a vacuum, however: those responsible are influenced by the intellectual and political climate and by the social and constitutional environment within which they operate. This chapter is concerned with the nature of those influences.

The principal intellectual influence upon legislators, as well as upon those appointed to implement their policies, has of course been economic theory. It would be difficult indeed to find another branch of public policy so thoroughly dominated by a set of abstract theoretical propositions. The original basis for competition policy was a set of propositions concerning competition which were first put forward by nineteenth-century economists; and those propositions continue to constitute what might be termed the 'mainstream view' of its rationale. They are founded, however, on a highly simplified model of the economy, and of the workings of firms within it; and even within that model, they are subject to important qualifications which are often overlooked. In recent years, moreover, the use of that model as the rationale for competition policy has come under attack, and fresh theoretical developments have begun to have their influence. Section B, below, is a non-technical résumé of the relevant propositions of mainstream competition theory and of its assumptions and limitations, together with a brief introduction to recent developments.

Competition policy need not, however, be exclusively concerned with the promotion of competition. Other objectives are also sought in the British system, and in most of the other regulatory systems. The choice of objectives can have a profound influence upon the practical working of a system, as can the choices which are made among the various possible modes of implementation. The system which is at present in operation in Britain is by no means immutable in those respects: several important changes are under consideration, and more may be forthcoming. The remainder of this chapter outlines the choices which are available to policy-makers in designing a regulatory system, and illustrates those choices with brief accounts of the differing approaches to regulation which have been taken in the United States, by the European Union and by the United Kingdom.

B   THE ECONOMIC RATIONALE

Perfect Competition

The merit of starting with the economists' concept of perfect competition is that it describes a situation which can readily be analysed to give some definite and straightforward answers. The concept refers, however, to a special set of circumstances which may in two senses be regarded as idealistic. In the first place, the circumstances themselves are so special that they are not often encountered in the real world. Secondly, the economic consequences of those circumstances turn out to be optimal in a precisely definable sense. Thus the imaginary world of perfect competition turns out also to be the best of all possible worlds.

The hypothetical world with which the concept of perfect competition is concerned is one in which the market for each category of product has the following characteristics.

- (a) *All market shares are small.* No supplier enjoys a share of the market which is large enough to enable him to influence the price of that category of product.
- (b) *No collusion.* Each supplier acts independently.
- (c) *No barriers to entry.* There is nothing to prevent any new supplier from entering the market for any category of product.
- (d) *Homogeneity of product.* All suppliers of each category of product are known by all buyers to supply identical products.

Suppliers are assumed to maximise their profits, and buyers are assumed to seek value for money. After a settling-down period, a market price emerges for each category of product. A supplier who attempts to sell a product at above that price will find no buyers, and a customer who attempts to buy a product at below that price will find no sellers.

Those characteristics define the conditions for perfect competition among suppliers of products. They may similarly be defined in relation to suppliers of labour. And for pure competition to apply to the market as a whole, conditions analogous to (a) and (b) must also be satisfied by buyers: there must be no dominant buyers, and buyers must not collude.

Economics textbooks analyse the consequences of perfect competition for buyers and for sellers (for example, Baumol, 1961). The term

'optimal resource allocation' is used to describe the theoretical outcome for the community as a whole. In non-technical language this
can be taken to mean the efficient allocation of resources as between
different categories of product. Perfect competition ensures that the
community's resources are used efficiently in the sense of making people
feel well-off. If resources are allocated efficiently, then people would
not, for example, feel better off if they were able to afford more meat
and less fish, nor vice versa. More precisely, the term means that there
can be no rearrangement of the allocation of resources which would
make anyone better off without making someone worse off.

A word of caution about terminology is needed at this point. The
temptation to assert that perfect competition maximises economic efficiency must be resisted. The theory outlined above makes purely
formal assumptions about productive efficiency, and thus does not deal
with factors influencing the efficiency with which resources are used
by individual suppliers to produce particular categories of product. Nor
is it strictly correct to say that perfect competition maximises economic welfare. The concept of economic welfare encompasses the way
in which wealth is distributed as between different members of the
community, and it cannot be claimed that perfect competition necessarily leads to an ideal distribution of wealth. The propositions which
emerge from the concept of perfect competition are to do with the
way in which resources are allocated between products, and not with
how the product is manufactured, or to whom it is distributed. (Readers
who wish to pursue the complications introduced by the concept of
economic welfare should consult Winch, 1971, or Little, 1957.)

Externalities

One further qualification is needed. The outcome will not necessarily
be efficient if any supplier can impose costs on others. In economics
jargon, these are termed 'externalities'. The conventional example is a
supplier who pollutes the environment. The allocation of resources need
not then be efficient because of the possibility that some people would
feel better off with fewer goods in exchange for a cleaner atmosphere.
Other examples include traffic congestion and mining subsidence. The
theoretically ideal solution is for the polluter to compensate those affected;
and if this is practicable, it takes the matter outside the scope of competition policy. Considerations of practicability may, however, occasionally require competition policy to take externalities into account
and to attempt to remedy the resulting distortion of consumer choice.

Perfect Monopoly and Oligopoly

The importance of the concept of perfect competition to the philosophy of competition policy is that it serves as a datum, or baseline, from which the departures which occur in the real world can be measured. It defines one of the polar extremes of possible real-world situations. The other polar extreme is perfect monopoly – that is to say a product market in which the product has only one supplier and into which no other supplier can enter. Like perfect competition, this is a situation which can readily be analysed to produce unequivocal results. The diagrammatic analysis which appears in the standard economic textbooks demonstrates that under these circumstances the profit-maximising supplier would provide smaller quantities of the product, and at a higher price, than would be the case under perfect competition.

The mechanism which leads to that unsurprising conclusion is of more interest than the conclusion itself. It rests on the fact that the monopolist always has the freedom to choose between supplying a greater quantity at a lower price and supplying a smaller quantity at a higher price (a freedom of choice which is represented in the textbook diagrams as a downward-sloping demand curve). If the monopolist maximises his profit, his choice is uniquely determined by the structure of his costs, taken together with the shape of the product demand curve (that is, the relationship between the price which he charges and the amount which can then be sold).

The existence of such choices is said to confer 'market power' upon the supplier in question. The possession of market power in that sense is not, however, confined to perfect monopolies. There are many markets in the real world in which there are several suppliers, each of which is large enough to enjoy a degree of market power in the sense of having some degree of choice concerning pricing policy. A great deal of theoretical work has been done on the subject but straightforward answers concerning the behaviour of a profit-maximising supplier in such an 'oligopolistic' market are hard to find. The reason is that analysis of such markets is complicated by the need to postulate how each supplier reacts to the likely behaviour of his competitors, and by the need for a precise understanding of each supplier's cost structure.

Since competition policy has to deal mainly with markets which operate under neither pure competition nor pure monopoly, these difficulties create a dilemma. Is it satisfactory to simplify the analysis by treating the real world as a mixture of many markets ruled by something approximating to perfect competition, together with a few others which approximate to pure monopoly? Or is it necessary to abandon that unrealistic simplification and tackle the formidable problems of ana-lysing oligopoly as it occurs in practice? In the post-war debate over this dilemma, the simplified approach was successfully defended by Professor Milton Friedman on the grounds that the value of any piece of analysis depends, not upon the realism of its underlying assump-tions, but upon its ability to yield useful results (Friedman, 1966). It was generally concluded that perfect competition and pure monopoly theory, applied with qualifications dictated by common sense, would yield a satisfactory theoretical basis for competition policy. That – at least, until recently – is how the matter was left.

The Second Best

Apart from the problems of living with the artificial assumptions under-lying conventional competition theory, there is one problem which is inherent in that theory. The theory's most telling conclusion is that if universal perfect competition is taken as the starting point, any depar-ture from it will lead to a loss of economic efficiency. But, if the starting point is one in which some markets are not perfectly competi-tive, it cannot be concluded that efficiency would be increased by re-storing any one of them to perfect competition. This is not a finicky academic point, moreover; it is a matter of some practical importance. It is not hard to see that it might be better from the consumer's stand-point to have a monopoly supplier of coal, faced with a monopoly supplier of electricity as his main customer, rather than an alternative in which the coal supplier would be free to exploit his monopoly power in dealings with a fragmented electricity supply industry. (The same problem can arise within a single market. In a market already domi-nated by a major supplier, a merger between two of that supplier's lesser rivals may make for an improvement of effective competition.)

The theory of the second best, as this is called, may seem seriously to undermine the intellectual foundations of competition policy, but in practice its implications are often less formidable. There is a clear need to take account of linkages between markets such as exist be-tween the markets for coal and electricity – and this can often be successfuly tackled by a mixture of analysis and common sense. Also, there are many instances in which such linkages are so weak that the direct benefits of an increase in competition in one market would clearly outweigh any adverse secondary effects. Cases are bound to arise, nonetheless, in which there is no analytical solution to the problem of the second best.

Policy Prescriptions

The economic rationale of competition policy which is set out in the above résumé has been concerned with what might be termed 'mainstream competition theory'. That mainstream theory does not, however, provide the only possible rationale for competition policy. A number of alternative theories of competition have been advanced over the years, some of which are now beginning to influence the conduct of competition policy. Since the practical relevance of those other strands of competition theory is determined by the extent to which they yield different policy prescriptions, the time has come to review the prescriptive implications of the mainstream theory.

Since departure from any of the four conditions for perfect competition listed on page 5, leads in theory to a loss of efficiency, the possible prescriptive implications of the theory might be categorised as follows.

(a) *Action to restrict market shares.* This might include controls on mergers, and the breaking-up of large firms.
(b) *Prohibition of collusion.* This could include the prohibition of any of a wide range of practices which limit competition among existing firms.
(c) *Removal of entry barriers.* Action could range from the prohibition of suppliers' practices which discourage entry, to positive action to promote entry.
(d) *Measures to improve information.* The measures might seek to prevent suppliers from misleading their customers, and they might also seek positively to inform customers.

In case of uncertainty concerning the effectiveness of the above, a fifth category would be:

(e) *Price control.* This would seek to compel a supplier to set prices at the levels which would rule under perfect competition.

The above are of course possible, not universal, prescriptions. Any of them may be rejected or modified for one of a number of reasons. Their rationale might be affected by externalities or by second-best considerations. The costs of the remedy may outweigh its benefits – as might easily be true of the breaking-up of a large firm. The regulatory authority may consider that it does not have the information or the competence to select an appropriate remedy, and may therefore do nothing for fear of making matters worse.

The Competitive Process

Critics have argued that the entire rationale of mainstream competition theory is flawed by virtue of its methodology. That methodology – which is termed 'comparative statics' – envisages a system which settles down to a stable equilibrium. The properties of that equilibrium are then analysed as though it were a static situation. In reality, of course, the postulated settling-down process may never end. New techniques and new products may emerge in a continuing stream; new firms may come into existence to turn the resulting opportunities into reality, and other firms may fail. Above all, there are uncertainties; and entrepreneurs are rewarded – if successful – for taking risks. None of those vital characteristics of the competitive process can be embodied in a comparative statics analysis. Consequently, it is argued, that form of analysis is inappropriate to the problem.

The principal proponents of that line of argument are the 'Austrian School' of economists, and their case is more extensively summarised in Littlechild (1986) and Reekie (1979).

A possible prescription for competition policy which follows from a full acceptance of the above argument is total inaction on the grounds that the analysis necessary for successful intervention is so complex, and the necessary information so hard to come by, that intervention is as likely to do harm as to do good. An alternative prescription is temporary inaction pending further analytical and empirical developments. The more pragmatic members of the Austrian School are prepared to countenance active competition policy, but counsel a cautious approach which recognises the complexity of the real world and the consequent dangers of error; and which therefore intervenes only in the most clear-cut of cases.

Contestability

Competition theory was augmented in the 1970s by analytical developments in which the concept of perfect competition was replaced as a benchmark by the concept of 'perfect contestability'. This has provided a new way of looking at competition.

A perfectly contestable market was defined as one into which entry is absolutely free *and* exit *is absolutely costless*. If the initial outlays required for entry to a market were recoverable without loss, then any risk which might otherwise attach to entry could be eliminated. A new supplier who could see a profitable opportunity of entering a market in which prices had previously been raised by the exercise of market power, would be aware that those prices would be likely to fall again as a result of his entry. But, given the opportunity of costless exit, that would not deter him from entering. There would be nothing to lose provided that he remained in the market for only so long as it continued to be profitable to do so. Faced by such a threat, a monopoly supplier in a perfectly contestable market would thus be deterred from setting his prices at above the level which would rule under perfect competition by the knowledge that to do so would be to encourage entry. If successful entry actually occurred, he would eventually be forced to reduce his prices to the level which would rule under perfect competition in order to survive.

A rigorous proof of those intuitively plausible propositions appears in Baumol (1982), and the topic is developed more fully in Baumol, Panzar and Willig (1982).

The policy implications of contestability have been explored by Baumol and others. If a market is found to be perfectly contestable – or nearly so – then the authorities need do nothing, and might do harm by intervening. If it is not fully contestable, then the preferred action is to attempt to remove the obstacles to contestability. If contestability cannot be guaranteed, however, there remains a case for applying the prescription of conventional competition theory. Any disadvantages of intervention – including, particularly, any discouragement offered to potential entrants – should, however, be carefully weighed against its likely benefits.

The practical implications of the theory of contestability have turned out to be very limited (as noted by Schwartz 1986). It was thought at first that perfect contestability might be closely approached in the real world. Promising examples were expected to be found in the deregulated United States airline industry – but investigations by Morrison and Winston (1987) and others have called this into question. It is clear that the existence of 'sunk costs' – such as the irrecoverable costs of promoting customer awareness of a new product – are a serious obstacle to contestability.

Limitations of the Rationale

Competition theory provides the intellectual foundation for competition policy but it does not provide all that is needed to build a serviceable structure upon that foundation. It does not lead to unequivocal prescriptions except where competition (and hence allocative efficiency) is the only question at issue – and even then the questions of externalities and of 'the second best' may introduce qualifications. Where the issue of gains in productive efficiency also arises, other branches of economic theory must be called in aid. The difficulties which then arise stem not so much from the limitations of the available theory, as from the fact that quantification is then needed in order to draw up a balance between losses of allocative efficiency and gains of productive efficiency. The analytical framework for such calculations is available, but the information requirements for a successful analysis tend to be demanding, and commercial accounting systems are seldom capable of providing the necessary inputs.

In practical terms, therefore, the economic rationale for competition policy is incomplete and, at best, its implementation depends partly upon judgement rather than entirely upon analysis. A very substantial programme of empirical work (such as that proposed by Baumol, Panzar and Willig, 1982, p. 467) would be needed to repair those deficiencies.

C   OBJECTIVES AND THEIR IMPLEMENTATION

The economic rationale which has been outlined above provides the intellectual justification for the proposition that competition policy can be used to increase economic efficiency. It does not, however, lead to any unique prescription for its implementation. As the following sections of this chapter will demonstrate, different administrations have developed widely differing systems of implementation, despite their common rationale. The differences arise from the choices which have been made concerning the range of objectives to be served, and concerning the means which may be chosen to achieve them.

Objectives

Competition theory indicates that individual businessmen may sometimes find it in their shareholders' interests to do things which are harmful to the community as a whole. If this were the only issue, and if intervention on behalf of the community could be confined to pro-hibiting those anti-competitive actions, then the choice of policy ob-jectives would be straightforward. The complicating factor is the possibility that some anti-competitive behaviour may not be unequivo-cally harmful.

It has been noted that the type of economic efficiency which, in competition theory, is diminished by a departure from pure competi-tion is 'allocative efficiency' – that is to say the efficiency with which resources are allocated as between alternative products; and that there may also be beneficial effects upon 'productive efficiency' – that is to say the efficiency with which resources are used within a firm or combine for the supply of particular products. (The rationale for the creation of a firm in the first place was probably the perception that productive efficiency could be increased by bringing together under one organisa-tion people who would otherwise be competing with each other in the market place.)

In formulating the objectives of policy, however, there may under some circumstances be a case for adopting the presumption that ef-fects on allocative efficiency will predominate unless the contrary can be demonstrated. In view of the analytical difficulties of demonstrat-ing where the balance lies, such a presumption can make it difficult – if not impossible – to defend any action which reduces competition. In the context of a heavily cartelised industry structure – such as was perceived to exist in the United States in the late nineteenth century – it might even seem sensible to concentrate upon improving allocative efficiency by attacking anti-competitive structures and practices, regard-less of any possible loss of productive efficiency. As will be seen, there are still some remnants of that approach in present-day United States anti-trust policy. To the extent that such a policy is successful, however, the case for persisting with it is weakened. A reaction against the ex-cesses which can arise under such a policy may lend plausibility to the opposite extreme of not intervening against a reduction of compe-tition unless action can be taken without any loss of productive efficiency.

If the promotion of competition is not to be the sole objective of competition policy, then other objectives must be formulated. The ob-jective need not of course be defined solely in terms of balancing allocative and productive efficiencies. A more ambitious objective would be to increase economic welfare – a concept which encompasses pro-ductive as well as allocative efficiency, but which also includes the controversial subject of the distribution of wealth. The lack of an objective criterion for wealth distribution might appear to be an obstacle to such

an extension of the economic objectives, but its place may be taken by
a social or political consensus in favour, for example, of greater equality,
the alleviation of unemployment, or the promotion of small firms.

The policy objectives need not be confined to economic goals; competition policy may be used also to promote wider social and political
objectives. To take an extreme case. British competition policy pur-
ports to promote 'the public interest' – a concept which embraces a
number of specified considerations, but which also leaves it to the
regulatory authority to take into account any further considerations as
it thinks fit. An unlimited objective of that sort is not, however, a real
choice; it represents a legislature's evasion of the need to make choices.
The need to set limits upon the objectives of competition policy cannot in fact be evaded; if they are not set by the legislature, they must
be set elsewhere. In the last resort, the appointed competition authorities may narrow the range of the objectives which they are prepared to consider in order to keep their investigations within practicable
limits. In the course of events, sight may then be lost of the prime
objective. In pursuit of an open-ended 'public interest', British competition policy has at times been used to promote political objectives
which conflict with the objective of promoting competition, such as a
desire to protect domestic suppliers or a desire to limit overseas control of domestic industries.

Rules, Discretion and Delegation

The chosen objectives may be sought either by the general enforcement of predetermined rules of conduct, or by a case-by-case exercise
of discretion. The constitutional traditions of western civilisation favour
rules-based enforcement because of its advantages in terms of transparency and accountability. The formulation of the legendary twelve
tables of Roman law is said to have been proposed by the tribune
Terentillus so that the ruling consuls would be 'bound to use against
the people only the authority granted to them by popular consent, instead of giving the force of law, as they do at present, to their own
arbitrary passions' (Livy). From the early days of the Roman Repub-
lic, lip-service at least has been given to the precept that government
may not interfere with the affairs of the citizen except on the basis of
a code of law which is accessible to all. Departures from that precept
have, however, been increasingly necessary because of the increasing
complexity of life and the consequent inability of legislatures to an-
ticipate all of the circumstances under which their legislation is to

apply. There nevertheless remains a constitutional presumption against the unnecessary use of discretionary methods of enforcement.

There are some business practices which can be regulated without difficulty by the enforcement of simple rules. Generally speaking, they consist of those easily defined practices which are considered to be harmful under all circumstances. But it is difficult to frame precise rules to deal with practices which are harmful only under particular circumstances, or only when carried to excess. Where matters of such complexity arise, some exercise of discretion is virtually inevitable. The choices which then remain are those concerning what limits are to be placed upon the exercise of that discretion, who is to exercise it, and what procedures they are to adopt.

In a system in which there is no statutory delegation of powers of discretion to ministers or to specialised agencies, it falls to the courts of law to exercise discretion on matters of substance as well as on matters of legal interpretation. Statutory delegation may be preferable where technical issues are involved which are considered to be beyond the competence of the courts. The delegation of statutory powers to agencies rather than to ministers can have the advantage of taking the exercise of discretion outside the scope of parliamentary debate, and thus of limiting the danger that decisions might be influenced by short-term political considerations. In the absence of parliamentary control, a measure of protection against the arbitrary, unfair, or irrational exercise of discretionary powers may be provided by a provision for appeal to the courts, but it is in the nature of the reasons for the appointment of a special agency that the courts would not normally overrule the agency on matters of professional judgement.

Where discretion is exercised by a statutory agency, that agency may be empowered within statutory limits to issue its own rules or guidelines, and its decisions may in time have the practical effect – if not the legal effect – of setting precedents. The true effect of the delegation of discretionary powers may thus be the eventual emergence of a well-founded and generally understood code of acceptable behaviour concerning a wide range of business practices.

Form and Effect

Whether rules-based or discretionary, a regulatory system requires clear definitions of the practices which fall within its scope. A practice may be defined for that purpose either in terms of its form, or in terms of its effect.

An example of the application of a form-based, or *per se*, definition would be the prohibition of exclusive dealing (the practice of making it a condition of supply that a retailer does not deal with other suppliers). A form-based definition of that sort has the merit of letting all concerned know exactly where they stand. It also simplifies regulation by excluding all considerations other than the evidence concerning the existence of the practice. However, it invites the use of devices which meet the letter of the law but evade its intent. A loyalty rebate could, in the example, be used to obtain the equivalent of exclusive dealing without breaching the form-based prohibition of that practice. An attempt to amend the form-based rules to prevent companies from evading the intent of the policy may result in an unending contest between the drafters of legislation and the company lawyers.

A prohibition of practices which have the *effect* of exclusive dealing could not be evaded in that way, and that alternative has the merit of directly attacking the real problem. On the other hand, the use of an effects-based prohibition introduces an element of judgement into the implementation of policy, which may reduce its certainty. The circumstances under which a quantity discount would be deemed to have the prohibited effect might, in the example, be unclear. In the longer term, however, many such uncertainties might be expected to be resolved by the establishment of precedents.

Structure and Behaviour

As in other contexts, there is also a choice between regulating structure and regulating conduct. The effectiveness of conduct regulation is limited by the fact that regulators have less knowledge than the regulated of internal factors such as costs, but other factors such as the advantages of large-scale operation may count against relying entirely upon the regulation of structure. In the context of competition policy that choice lies between the alternatives of limiting the acquisition of market power, or of preventing the abuse of market power once it has been acquired. Regulatory systems whose objectives are concerned exclusively with the promotion of competition are likely to implement that objective mainly by stringent control upon mergers and by the breaking up of existing monopolies. Where the objectives also include the promotion of productive efficiency, account is likely to be taken of the benefits of mergers and of the costs of disruption. The more permissive attitude toward mergers which such objectives imply may require a correspondingly severe attitude toward the abuse of market power, with the practical difficulties which that implies.

Predictability and Effectiveness

The effectiveness of a regulatory system may largely depend upon how well the various options which are available for its implementation are matched to the situations to which they are applied. For example, an attempt to regulate a complex situation by means of simple form-based rules may be expected to produce erratic results, while a discretionary effects-based system may be a cumbersome way of dealing with simpler situations. Within any given system, however, it is the conduct of the regulatory authorities that is likely to be the crucial factor. Erratic and unpredictable conduct on their part can limit the effectiveness of the system, besides imposing unnecessary costs upon business. A pattern of conduct which conveys clear signals to businessmen can, on the other hand, bring customary business behaviour more closely into line with policy objectives, and thus reduce the need for further intervention.

The solution to the problem of how to regulate the regulators would therefore seem to depend upon a periodical review of the effects of their decisions upon the perceptions of businessmen, and of the likely consequences of those perceptions for the community as a whole.

D   THE UNITED STATES APPROACH

Although United States antitrust policy differs in important respects from British competition policy, it has had a strong influence upon the development of policy in Britain. When the present framework of competition policy was being created in post-war Britain, its legislators had before them the record of fifty years of operation of United States policy to serve as an example and a warning. Whatever its strengths and weaknesses, the American system has behind it an incomparable wealth of practical experience and analytical development. The atmosphere of political controversy which has often surrounded the subject in the United States has also served as a stimulus to its intellectual development, to an extent which is unparalleled elsewhere. Consequently, the bulk of the literature on competition policy is of American origin, and the ideas, terminology and methods of analysis which originated there are a vital part of the background to British and European thinking.

The inclusion in this chapter of a brief review of the antitrust system thus serves to illustrate the possible consequences of some of the available choices of objectives and methods of implementation of competition policy. With British policy in the course of transition, it also provides examples of how some of the alternatives to the existing system might be expected to work.

The Sherman Act and the Rule of Reason

The term 'antitrust' originated from the nineteenth-century practice of placing the stock of a large number of competing companies into the hands of trustees who were then able to restrict competition in that industry. Public indignation at that and other perceived abuses by big business led to the passing in 1890 of the Sherman Act. That legislation condemned such practices in stark and uncompromising terms:

> Every contract, combination in the form of trust . . . or otherwise, or conspiracy in restraint of trade . . . is hereby declared illegal . . . Every person who shall monopolise or attempt to monopolise . . . any part of trade or commerce shall be deemed guilty of a felony.

Practices falling within either of those broad categories thus became criminal offences. Initially, however, the Act was found to be unworkable. Its form-based prohibitions were so general as to catch a wide range of established and harmless business practices. Supreme Court interpretations eventually provided workable interpretations by introducing 'the rule of reason', under which certain forms of business behaviour could be judged, not solely by their form, but also by their effects or by the intent of the parties concerned. Nevertheless, a wide range of business practices, including price-fixing agreements, market sharing, and refusal to supply, continue to be deemed to be illegal *per se* – so that proof of their existence is sufficient to secure a conviction, and no defence relating to their effects is allowable.

The Sherman Act was supplemented in 1914 by the more specific terms of the Clayton Act. Among practices made unlawful under that act were price discrimination, exclusive dealing, tie-in sales, and interlocking directorates – subject in each case to the condition that the purpose or effect of the practice would be 'substantially to lessen competition'. Section 2, dealing with price discrimination, was amended in 1936 by the Robinson–Patman Act, which made it unlawful to discriminate in price between different purchasers of goods of like grade and quality where the effect would be substantially to lessen competition (unless the price differentials would only compensate for differences in costs of supply). Section 7 of the Clayton Act, as amended in 1950, prohibited mergers which would substantially lessen competition. The Clayton Act and its amendments do not create criminal offences.

Objectives and Interpretations

Supreme Court interpretations have attributed objectives to the legislators of the Sherman Act which go beyond the pursuit of economic efficiency. For example, Judge Learned Hand said that:

> great industrial consolidations are undesirable regardless of their economic results . . . among the purposes of Congress in 1890 was a desire to put an end to great aggregations of capital because of the helplessness of the individual before them. (*ALCOA 1945*)

– and in 1962 the Supreme Court attributed to Congress the policy of 'protecting viable, small, locally owned businesses . . . even at the expense of occasional higher costs and prices' (*Brown Shoe* 1962).

The use of competition policy to attack big business and to protect small firms continued to be a feature of the US approach until appointees of the Reagan Administration took steps to limit that use of antitrust policy.

The actual wording of the antitrust legislation is, however, exclusively concerned with competition and, until 1977, it was interpreted to exclude consideration of offsetting gains in productive efficiency. In one merger case, the Supreme Court went so far as to rule that not only were gains in productive efficiency no defence, but that they could actually be used to attack a merger proposal since small rivals could be damaged thereby (*Brown Shoe*, 1962). In 1977, the Supreme Court overruled previous precedents and accepted that gains in the efficiency of distribution provided a valid defence of locational restrictions under a franchising arrangement (*Sylvania*, 1977). It would appear, however that no such defence is permitted for resale price maintenance, which therefore remains illegal.

Despite its preoccupation with practices which would give power to raise prices, the charging of excessive prices does not in itself attract disapproval under US antitrust law. In one case, indeed, the Court of Appeals ruled that excessive pricing is pro-competitive in view of the incentive it provides to new entrants (*Berkey Photo* 1979). In other cases the courts have shown a strong reluctance to put themselves in the position of price regulators.

The burden of proof that a merger would not harm competition falls at present upon its proponents, and the mere possibility that there might be even a very small reduction of competition has in the past been sufficient to justify prohibition. Merger Guidelines issued by the Department of Justice provide for reasonably precise criteria which take account of market shares, ease of entry and efficiency gains.

The Proposals of the Chicago School

Thus, although the US antitrust system operates in principle on the basis of legal precedents, those precedents have not presented a consistent philosophy and they have on occasion been overruled. Some of the Supreme Court's decisions have been strongly attacked by economists and lawyers of the 'Chicago School' who, under the Reagan Administration, came to occupy influential positions in the Department of Justice. The Chicago School are particularly critical of judgements based upon antipathy to big business, and of those which neglected the benefits to consumers from gains in productive efficiency. They advocate a move to a wholly effects-based system in which the economic welfare of consumers would be the sole criterion. (Economic welfare in that sense is however interpreted narrowly to include only effects on prices and consumer choice. The idea of adopting a broadly defined 'public interest' criterion is firmly rejected.) Some members of the Chicago School have put forward analytical procedures for determining the tradeoff between losses of allocative efficiency resulting from restrictions upon competition, and offsetting gains in productive efficiency (for example, Williamson 1987, Chapter 1). Others have argued that the task of measuring efficiency is itself impossible, and that all agreements which are 'ancilliary to an integration of productive economic activity' should be permitted – including resale price maintenance (Bork 1978 pp. 125, 406).

The main influence of the Chicago School upon competition policy under the Reagan administration was a strong reluctance to take action against 'vertical' restrictions imposed by sellers upon buyers (such as making the purchase of one product conditional upon the purchase of others). There have since been signs of a reversal of that policy under the Bush and Clinton administrations.

Enforcement and Effectiveness

The effectiveness of US antitrust law owes much to its methods of enforcement. A violation of the Sherman Act is a criminal offence, punishable by fines or imprisonment. Injunctions may be granted by the courts under that and other antitrust legislation, to prevent anti-competitive behaviour or to require divestiture of parts of a monopoly. Injured parties may bring actions for 'triple damages', that is to say compensation amounting to three times the amount of the damage actually sustained. Taken together with legal presumptions which often tend to go against the defendant, these are powerful deterrents.

Notwithstanding the controversy about the total economic effect of antitrust, there can be no denying its effectiveness in promoting competition. The breaking up of giant corporations such as Standard Oil and IT&T are among its more dramatic achievements, and it has undoubtedly had a pervasive effect upon business behaviour throughout the United States.

E THE EUROPEAN UNION APPROACH

The European Union approach, like the United States approach, offers a practical example of the operation of competition policy in ways that might be considered as alternatives to some features of the British approach. It is also of more direct interest because of the way that it impinges directly upon the behaviour of British businessmen. The account of it given below is very brief in view of the detailed treatment which it receives in later chapters.

In its approach to market power, EU policy contrasts somewhat with that of the United States. The latter, as has been seen, seeks primarily to prevent monopolisation. In contrast, the competition legislation of the Treaty of Rome was concerned with the abuse of monopoly power rather than its existence. Subsequent interpretations established, however, that a merger which increases the market power of a dominant firm could itself be condemned as an abuse, and further legislation provided for the prohibition of any merger which creates or strengthens a dominant position and so restricts competition. Agreements between firms and other 'concerted practices' which restrict competition may also be prohibited. Thus EU policy acts against both the restriction of competition and the abuse of market power.

The objectives of EU policy are not defined with any precision in its legislation but it is clear that they do not extend to a concern for bigness, as in the US approach. The treatment of concerted practices is not directed exclusively at their effects upon competition and allocative efficiency: the legislation provides specifically for exemption on the grounds of beneficial effects upon productive efficiency.

The EU operates an effects-based discretionary system under which breaches of its rules can be punished by fines. The uncertainties which are bound to exist in the early years of a discretionary system have been substantially narrowed by the issue of guidelines and block exemptions, and by the precedents of the European Courts, which together provide a detailed, if incomplete, code of business behaviour.

F   THE UNITED KINGDOM APPROACH

United Kingdom competition policy has been developed in a piecemeal fashion over the post-war years, and it is now undergoing a further period of change. This applies particularly to the open-ended 'public interest' criterion which, until recently, has constituted the only formal statement of its objectives. The public interest is defined in the legislation to include the promotion of competition and matters concerning prices and consumer choice, but also to include the promotion of regional policy and of exports, and any other matters which appear to be relevant. The breadth of that criterion has in the past enabled the competition authorities to be concerned with a number of cases which raised no significant competition issues. As the following chapters will indicate, the UK approach is now concerned mainly – but not exclusively – with cases in which the main issue is the promotion of competition.

As a result of the piecemeal nature of its development the present UK approach to restrictive practices differs radically from the approach taken to other aspects of competition policy.

Restrictive Practices

Collectively enforced resale price maintenance is unlawful, and a comprehensive range of other collectively enforced restrictions are presumed to be against the public interest unless they can be shown to meet specific criteria. Rebuttal of that presumption has proved to be so difficult that its practical effect has been to prohibit all such practices, except in a few special cases. (The same is true of individually enforced resale price maintenance.) There is a requirement to register restrictive practices falling within the scope of the legislation, but failure to do so carries no penalties, and the authorities' powers of detection are limited. Penalties for contempt of court can be levied against those who disregard a prohibition. The courts have threatened but never implemented the imprisonment of directors, and really substantial financial penalties have been rare.

Thus the present UK system of dealing with concerted practices amounts in effect to a form-based prohibition without penalties.

Monopolies, Mergers and Anti-Competitive Practices

In contrast to its approach to concerted practices and resale price maintenance, British legislation makes no presumption concerning the effect on the public interest of monopolies and mergers. The jurisdiction of the competition authorities over monopolies and mergers is limited by form-based rules relating to size or market share, but within those limits the policy is implemented by a discretionary effects-based system. Decisions concerning effects on the public interest are not considered to create legal precedents and no guidelines are available to indicate what is, or is not, deemed to be against the public interest. There are no penalties except for breach of an order to desist, and no provision for private civil actions. A similar approach is taken to individually enforced anti-competitive practices.

2 The Legislative Framework

A INTRODUCTION

British and EU legislation set the framework within which competition policy operates in Britain. EU law takes precedence over British law, but is concerned only with matters which may affect trade between member states (a business which trades only within Britain is not, however, exempt from the provisions of EU law if its conduct could have an effect upon imports from other member states). Thus there remain large areas of domestic trade and commerce which are subject only to national competition legislation. In other areas, the existence of two systems of legislation raises the possibility of conflicts and inconsistencies.

British and EU competition laws are framed in terms which are often too broad to convey to business executives more than the most general indication of what is expected of them. Their main purpose is to set up regulatory agencies, to define the limits of their operation, to provide them with broad objectives and guidelines, and to determine their procedures. What little the legislation has to say about business practices is nevertheless a major influence on the conduct of the regulatory authorities.

This chapter sets out the statutory objectives of the legislation and paraphrases for reference purposes its specific provisions concerning business structure and practices. Its provisions concerning the appointment of regulatory agencies and their procedures are dealt with in the next chapter, and questions of interpretation are examined in Part II.

Objectives

The objective of the EU's competition policy, as stated in Article 3 of the Treaty of Rome is that of 'ensuring that competition in the Common Market is not distorted'. That objective, together with the other provisions of the Treaty of Rome, was embodied in British law by virtue of the European Communities Act 1972.

The statutory objectives of Britain's national competition policy are contained in the definitions of the public interest in the Fair Trading Act 1973, the Restrictive Trade Practices Act 1976 and the Resale

TABLE 1   *Public interest criteria*

FT   denotes objective under s84 of the Fair Trading Act 1973
RTP   denotes defence under s10 of the Restrictive Trade Practices Act
       1976
RP   denotes defence under s14 of the Resale Prices Act 1976

Competition
FT: Promoting effective competition between suppliers.
       Facilitating entry of new competitors.
RTP: Necessary to counteract measures to restrict competition or to get
       fair terms with dominant supplier.
RP: Removal would reduce number of sales outlets.

Consumer benefits
FT: Promoting the interests of users in respect of prices, quality and
       variety.
RTP: Removal would deny substantial benefits to consumers.
RP: Removal would lead to price increases or reductions in quality and
       variety of goods, or in-service and after-sales service.

Productive efficiency
FT: Promoting through competition, reductions in costs, and new
       techniques and products.

Employment
FT: Promoting the balanced distribution of industry and employment.
RTP: Removal would have serious and persistent adverse effect on the
       general level of unemployment.

Exports
FT: Promoting competitive activity by UK companies in markets outside
       the UK.
RTP: Removal would cause a reduction in export business.

Health and safety
RTP: Necessary to protect the public against injury.
RP: Removal likely to cause danger to health.

Prices Act 1976. The various components of those definitions are set
out in summary form in Table 1. (Their precise relevance to particular
practices is explained under the appropriate headings below.)

The remainder of this chapter is intended to do no more than provide a convenient index to those parts of the legislation which deal
with business practices and structures, and give a concise survey of
their substance. The terminology of the legislation is abridged or

simplified where it is necessary to serve those purposes. The relevant material is assembled under seven headings as follows:

- B   Restrictive practices
- C   Monopolies
- D   Competition Act and general references
- E   Restrictive labour practices
- F   Mergers and joint ventures
- G   Patents and copyrights
- H   State-controlled enterprises and public utilities

Abbreviations throughout are:

FTA – The Fair Trading Act 1973
RTP Act – The Restrictive Trade Practices Act 1976
RP Act – The Resale Prices Act 1976
Comp Act – The Competition Act 1980
Article – A clause of the Treaty of Rome
Regulation – A European Community regulation.

B   RESTRICTIVE PRACTICES

European Union Law

The Treaty of Rome prohibits as incompatible with the common market:

all agreements between undertakings, decisions by associations of undertakings and concerted practices which may affect trade between member states and which have as their object or effect the prevention, restriction or distortion of competition within the common market, and in particular those which:
 (a) directly or indirectly fix purchase or selling prices or any other trading conditions;
 (b) limit or control production, markets, technical development or investment;
 (c) share markets or sources of supply;
 (d) apply dissimilar conditions to equivalent transactions with other trading parties, thereby placing them at a competitive disadvantage;
 (e) make the conclusion of contracts subject to acceptance by the

other parties of supplementary obligations which, by their nature or according to commercial usage, have no connection with the subject of such contracts.

(Article 85(1))

Any such agreements are automatically void.

(Article 85(2))

Breaches of the prohibition may attract fines of up to ten per cent of turnover, and periodic penalties may be imposed for continuing breaches.
(Articles 16 & 17 of Regulation 17)

Exemptions under European Union Law

The above provisions may be declared inapplicable where the practice:

contributes to improving the production or distribution of goods or to promoting technical or economic progress, while allowing consumers a fair share of the resulting benefit, and does not:
 (a) impose on the undertakings concerned restrictions which are not indispensable to the attainment of those objectives;
 (b) afford such undertakings the possibility of eliminating competition in respect of a substantial part of the products in question.

(Article 85(3))

Where individual exemption is required under Article 85(3), the practice must be notified to the Commission, except in the case of certain bilateral agreements relating to standards, joint R&D or specialisation, and single-country practices which do not relate to trade between member states.
(Regulation 17)

The Commission has advised that agreements need not be notified if they are concerned with goods or services which do not represent more than 5 per cent of the market in the area of the common market covered by the agreement, and the aggregate annual turnover of the parties to the agreement does not exceed 300 million ECU.

Block exemptions under specified conditions have been granted for:

(a) bilateral exclusive distribution agreements;
(Regulation 1983/83)**

(b) bilateral exclusive purchasing agreements; (with special rules for the supply of beer and petrol)

(Regulation 1984/83)**

(c) bilateral patent licensing agreements;

(Regulation 2349/84)*

(d) bilateral know-how licensing agreements;

(Regulation 556/89)*

(e) selective distribution for motor vehicles;

(Regulation 123/85)

(f) specialisation agreements;

(Regulation 417/85)*

(g) research and development agreements;

(Regulation 418/84)*

(h) bilateral franchise agreements;

(Regulation 4087/88)

(i) insurance agreements.

(Regulation 1534/91)

* as amended by Regulation 151/93
** as amended by Commission Notice 1992

Special exemptions have also been granted for certain agreements involving road, sea and air transport undertakings.

United Kingdom Law

The Restrictive Trade Practices Act 1976 requires the notification of all agreements concerning the production or supply of goods under which restrictions are accepted in respect of:

(a) the prices to be charged, quoted or paid, or for the application of any process of manufacture;
(b) the prices to be recommended for resale;
(c) the terms or conditions subject to which goods are to be supplied or acquired or any such process is to be applied;
(d) the quantities or descriptions of goods to be produced, supplied or acquired;
(e) the processes of manufacture to be applied, or the quantities or descriptions of goods to which any such process is to be applied;
(f) the persons or classes of persons to whom goods are to be supplied or from whom they are to be acquired, or the places in or from

which goods are to be supplied or acquired, or any such process applied.

(Section 6(1) RTP Act)

The requirement applies to restrictive agreements concerning services, defined in similar terms (except for (b) above) and also to agreements to share information concerning the cost of producing goods and services.

(Section 7, 11 & 12 RTP Act)

Restrictions contained in unregistered agreements are void and unlawful, and a restriction becomes void and is prohibited if the Restrictive Practices Court finds it to be against the public interest. There are no criminal penalties for failure to register a registrable agreement, but parties to such an agreement are subject to actions in the civil courts.

(Sections 2 & 35 RTP Act)

The Restrictive Practices Court is required to find the relevant part of an agreement to be against the public interest unless it accepts one or more of the specific defences summarised in Table 1, and is further satisfied that the practice is:

not unreasonable having regard to the balance between those circumstances and any detriment to persons not party to the agreement.

(Section 10 RTP Act)

Exceptions under United Kingdom Law

Excluded from the Act are:

(a) a very wide range of professional services;

(Schedule 1 RTP Act)

(b) bilateral exclusive dealing agreements; and,

(c) copyright and patent licences, trade marks and bilateral know-how agreements;

(Schedule 3 RTP Act)

(d) agreements involving agricultural marketing boards etc and agreements involving transport undertakings;

(Agriculture Act 1970 and various statutory instruments)

(e) the Stock Exchange;

(The RTP Stock Exchange Act 1984)

(f) agreements important to the national economy and approved by
the order of the Secretary of State;
(Section 29 RTP Act)

(g) a large number of agreements concerning particular organisations (for a list, see DTI1988, Annex D).

Notification is no longer required from companies with a turnover of
less than £5 million or with a market share of less than 5 per cent, or
for agreements meeting the criteria of current European Union block
exemptions, but the Director-General can call for details of any such
agreement and put it on the register if he considers its competition
effects to be significant.
(Deregulation and Contracting Out Act 1994)

C MONOPOLIES

European Union Law

The Treaty of Rome prohibits as incompatible with the common market:

any abuse by one or more undertakings of a dominant position within
the common market or in a substantial part of it ... in so far as it
may affect trade between member states. Such abuse may in particular consist in:

(a) directly or indirectly imposing unfair purchase or selling prices
or unfair trading conditions;

(b) limiting production, markets or technical development to the
prejudice of consumers;

(c) applying dissimilar conditions to equivalent transactions with
other trading parties, thereby placing them at a competitive
disadvantage;

(d) making the conclusion of contracts subject to acceptance by
the other parties of supplementary obligations which, by their
nature or according to commercial usage, have no connection
with the subject of such contracts.
(Article 86)

United Kingdom Law

The Fair Trading Act 1973 provides for inquiries to determine whether a statutory 'monopoly situation' (as defined below) exists and if so whether any act or omission on the part of those concerned operates or may be expected to operate against the public interest (as defined in Table 1 above).

Definition of a 'Monopoly Situation'
A monopoly situation in relation to the supply of goods is taken to exist if:

(a) at least one quarter of all the goods of any description which are supplied in the United Kingdom are supplied by one and the same person, or are supplied to one and the same person, or

(b) at least one quarter of all the goods of any description which are supplied in the United Kingdom are supplied by members of one and the same group of interconnected bodies corporate, or are supplied to members of one and the same group of interconnected bodies corporate, or

(c) at least one quarter of all the goods of any description which are supplied in the United Kingdom are supplied by members of one and the same group constituting a 'complex monopoly' (as defined below) or are supplied to members of one and the same such group, or

(d) one or more agreements are in operation, the result of which is that goods of any description are not supplied in the United Kingdom at all.

(Section 6(1) FTA)

Definition of a 'Complex Monopoly'
A complex monopoly is taken to exist if the members of the group referred to in (c) above, so conduct their affairs – whether voluntarily or not, and whether by agreement or not – as in any way to prevent, restrict or distort competition in connection with the production of goods or the supply of services, whether or not they themselves are affected by the competition and whether the competition is between persons interested as producers or suppliers or between persons interested as customers of producers or suppliers.

(Sections 6(2) & 7(2) FTA)

A monopoly situation is taken to exist in relation to the exports of goods of any description if:

(a) at least one quarter of the goods of that description are produced by a person or by members of a group as defined in (a) or (b) above (in which case the monopoly situation is taken to exist both for exports of goods of that description from the United Kingdom generally and for the exports of those goods to each market taken separately); or,

(b) there are agreements in operation, concerning at least one quarter of those goods which are produced in the United Kingdom, which in any way prevent restrict or distort competition in export markets.

(Section 8 FTA)

A monopoly situation in relation to the supply of services in the United Kingdom is defined in the same terms as for the supply of goods above, except that services may be treated as supplied in the United Kingdom if the supplier:

(a) has a place of business in the United Kingdom, or
(b) controls the relevant activities from the United Kingdom, or
(c) being a body corporate, is incorporated under the law of Great Britain or of Northern Ireland.

(Section 7 FTA)

D   COMPETITION ACT AND GENERAL REFERENCES

Competition Act References

As noted above, restrictive practices by dominant firms which do not fall within the scope of the Restrictive Trade Practices Act may be dealt with under British law by a monopoly reference under the Fair Trading Act. Alternatively, they may be dealt with as anti-competitive practices under the Competition Act 1980.

An anti-competitive practice is defined in the Competition Act as:

a course of conduct which of itself or when taken together with a course of conduct pursued by persons associated with him, has or is intended to have or is likely to have the effect of restricting, distorting or preventing competition in connection with the production, supply or acquisition of goods in the United Kingdom or any part of it or the supply or securing of services in the United Kingdom or any part of it.

(Section 2 Comp Act)

The Act provides for a reference to the Monopolies and Mergers Commission requiring it to conclude whether in its view the practice is anticompetitive, and if so whether it is against the public interest. The Act enables undertakings to be sought from those concerned, or for prohibition of the practice if it is found to be against the public interest.

A practice cannot, however, be investigated if:

(a) it is carried out by a firm with an annual turnover of less than £10 million and which has less than a 25 per cent share of a relevant market, and which is not a member of a group with either an annual turnover of £10 million or more and which has a 25 per cent share or more of a relevant market; or,

(b) it is carried out in certain exempted sectors, such as international shipping and international civil aviation; or,

(c) it arises from a registrable agreement under the Restrictive Trade Practices Act.

(The Anti-Competitive Practices (Exclusions) Order 1980 as amended by the Anti-Competitive Practices (Exclusions) (Amendment) Order 1994)

General References

Particular classes of practices, such as discounts to retailers and the restrictions upon advertising by solicitors, may be investigated at the request of the Secretary of State to determine their effect on the public interest under the provisions of the Fair Trading Act 1973, where they are:

(a) practices of a specified class which in his opinion are commonly adopted as a result of, or for the purpose of preserving, monopoly situations, or

(b) practices which appear to him to be uncompetitive practices

The report of the inquiry may, if required, include recommendations concerning remedial action, but the Act does not itself empower the Secretary of State to apply any remedy. The purpose of initiating such inquiries is normally to get advice concerning the advisability of making legislative changes. (Such inquiries need not be confined to individual practices, but may include practices exempted from consideration under the Restrictive Trade Practices Act.)

(Section 78 FTA)

E RESTRICTIVE LABOUR PRACTICES

European Union Law

It is generally held that the activities of employees and of trade unions in connection with industrial relations fall outside the scope of Article 85 of the Treaty of Rome (Bellamy and Child 1987 p. 47). If so, it would appear that there is no legislation concerning restrictive labour practices.

United Kingdom Law

For the purpose of the Fair Trading Act 1973, a restrictive labour practice is defined as:

> any practice whereby restrictions or other requirements, not ... relating exclusively to rates of remuneration, operate in relation to the employment of workers in any commercial activities in the United Kingdom or in relation to work done by any such workers, and are restrictions or requirements which –
> (a) could be discontinued without thereby contravening the provisions of an enactment or of any instrument having effect by virtue of an enactment, and
> (b) are not necessary for, or are more stringent than is necessary for, the efficient conduct of those activities.

(Section 79(5) FTA)

The Act provides for investigations to determine whether such practices exist generally or in relation to specified commercial activities, and if so whether they are against the public interest. Actions in contemplation of or furtherance of an industrial dispute are to be excluded from any such inquiry. The Act does not provide for the recommendation of remedies for practices found to be against the public interest, and does not empower the Secretary of State to apply remedies. Like the general references referred to above, its purpose in this connection is to obtain information and advice.

F   MERGERS AND JOINT VENTURES

European Union Law

Mergers

A 'concentration' is deemed to arise where two or more previously independent undertakings merge.

A concentration having a 'community dimension' (as defined in section B of Chapter 6 below) must be notified to the Commission and will be prohibited if, in the Commission's opinion it

> creates or strengthens a dominant position as a result of which effective competition would be significantly impeded in the common market or in a substantial part of it.

> **Art 2(3) Regulation 4064/89**

Joint Ventures

A concentration is also deemed to arise where

- one or more persons already controlling at least one undertaking, or
- one or more undertakings

acquire, whether by purchase of securities or assets, by contract or by any other means, direct or indirect control of the whole or parts of one or more other undertakings.

A joint venture is, however, deemed to create a concentration only if

   (a) it performs on a lasting basis all the functions of an autonomous economic entity; and,
   (b) it does not give rise to coordination of competitive behaviour of the parties amongst themselves or between them and the joint venture.

(Supplement 2/90 of the Bulletin of the European Communities contains a Commission Notice explaining these requirements.)

Joint ventures fulfilling the above conditions are termed *concentrative* and are treated in the same way as mergers. Otherwise they are termed *cooperative* and may fall under the provisions of Article 85 of the Treaty.

United Kingdom Law

A merger situation qualifying for investigation is taken to occur if two
or more enterprises cease to be distinct enterprises (as defined below),
at least one of which was carried on in the United Kingdom or under
the control of a body corporate incorporated in the United Kingdom
and if either:

(a) those enterprises would together supply or receive at least one
quarter of the goods or services of a particular description supplied in the United Kingdom or a substantial part of it; or,

(b) the value of the assets taken over exceeds £70 million.

(Section 64 FTA)

Enterprises are taken to cease to be distinct enterprises if either:

(a) they are brought under common ownership or common control
(as defined below) – whether or not the business to which either
of them formerly belonged continues to be carried on under the
same or different ownership or control – or,

(b) either of the enterprises ceases to be carried on at all and does
so in consequence of any arrangements or transaction entered
into to prevent competition between the enterprises.

Enterprises are taken to be under 'common control' if they are:

(a) enterprises of interconnected bodies corporate; or,

(b) enterprises carried on by two or more bodies corporate of which
one and the same person or group of persons has control (as
defined below); or,

(c) an enterprise carried on by a body corporate and an enterprise
carried on by a person or group of persons having control of
that body corporate.

A person is regarded as 'having control' of an enterprise if he is
able directly or indirectly materially to influence the policy of that
enterprise, although not having a controlling interest in it.

(Section 65 FTA)

(Note: interpretation of this provision is discussed in section B of Chapter 6.)

If as a result of a reference to the Monopolies and Mergers Commission, a merger situation qualifying for investigation is found to exist and it is found that it operates or may be expected to operate against the public interest (as defined in Table 1) the Secretary of State is empowered to take action to remedy or prevent any adverse effects specified in the Commission's report.

(Section 73 FTA)

There are also special provisions concerning newspaper mergers.

(Section 57–62 FTA)

Parties to a merger referred to the Commission may not acquire each other's shares without the permission of the Secretary of State.

(Companies Act 1989)

G   PATENTS AND COPYRIGHTS

European Union Law

There is as yet no operative Community legislation governing the issue of patents. The Community Patent Convention, when it comes into effect, will enable community-wide patents to be issued. Its legislative authority in Britain is provided by s86–88 of the Patents Act 1977. In the meantime, the European Patents Convention enables the European Patent Office at Munich to issue bundles of national patents, thus removing the need for a patentee to take out individual patents in every member state. It was implemented in Britain by S77–85 of the Patents Act 1977.

The use of national patents, copyrights, and so on, to restrict the import of goods from other member states is, however, regulated by the Treaty of Rome:

Quantitative restrictions on imports, and all measures having equivalent effect shall without prejudice to the following provisions, be prohibited between member states.

(Article 30)

Among the provisions referred to is:

The provisions of Article 30 ... shall not preclude prohibitions or restrictions on imports . . . justified on the grounds of . . . the protection of industrial or commercial property. Such prohibitions or restrictions shall not, however, constitute a means of arbitrary discrimination or a disguised restriction on trade between member states.

(Article 36)

Elsewhere, the treaty also provides that:

The Treaty shall in no way prejudice the rules in member states governing the system of property ownership.

Patent licensing agreements are also regulated by Article 85 of the Treaty, subject to a block exemption covering agreements under which:

(a) only two undertakings are party;
(b) the licensor grants a qualified exclusive licence; and,
(c) the licensee accepts certain limitations on his freedom actively to promote or to sell the licensed product elsewhere in the Community.

(Regulation 2349/84)

United Kingdom Law

United Kingdom law concerning intellectual property rights had, until recently, become anomalous as a result of judicial interpretations, and had lacked a consistent means of balancing the public interest in promoting competition against the public interest in promoting creativity and innovation. The legislation now enables the Secretary of State to take action to restrict the exercise of an intellectual property right in any case in which the Monopolies and Mergers Commission makes an adverse public interest finding on the grounds that its owner had refused to grant licences on reasonable terms, or that a licence had placed unreasonable restrictions upon the licensee.

The following paragraphs provide a brief guide to the main features of the legislation which now governs the four categories of intellectual property right under United Kingdom law:

(a) Patents
   A patentable invention has to be a new and non-obvious idea 'capable of industrial exploitation'. Essentially artistic or

intellectual matters are excluded. The right to apply for a patent belongs to the owner of the invention – the inventor himself or anyone who can claim the invention from him. A patent lasts – so long as renewal fees are paid – for 20 years from the date when the full specification of the invention is filed at the Patent Office. It is not fully effective until publication by that office – about 18 months from when the patent is applied for. The patentee obtains the exclusive right to use the idea, subject to the public interest conditions described above.

(The Patents Act 1977)

(b) Copyrights

A copyright is a property right in an original literary, dramatic, musical or artistic work, or in a film, sound recording, broadcast, or typographical arrangement of a published edition. Design documents (e.g., drawings) may be included, but it is not an infringement of a copyright to make or copy an article to such a design, unless the design is an artistic work or a typeface. The copyright belongs automatically to the author or to anyone to whom he assigns it. A copyright lasts for 50 years after the death of the author, or – in the case of films, recordings etc. – for 50 years after the date of release, or – in the case of typographical arrangements – for 25 years after publication. As for a patentee, the owner of a copyright obtains exclusive rights over the work, subject to the public interest conditions which have been referred to. (There are, however some minor exceptions concerning students, reviewers, librarians, etc.).

(The Copyright, Designs and Patents Act 1988)

(c) Design rights

A design right is a property right in an original design which defines the physical shape of an article. It gives its owner exclusive rights, not only over the design document but also over articles made to that design. Those rights are subject to the same public interest conditions as for patents and copyrights. The design right is owned by the designer if he was working independently, and otherwise to the person who commissioned or employed him to produce the design. A design right lasts – either for 15 years from the end of the year in which the design is first recorded or an article is first made to the design (whichever happens first) – or for ten years from the end of the year in which articles to the design are first put on sale or hire, if that happens within five years from the time when the design was re-corded or the first article made.

(The Copyright, Designs and Patents Act 1988)

(d) Registered designs

A design may be registered by its owner if it is new and it defines the shape or appearance of an article whose appeal is essentially aesthetic and not purely functional. Registration is essentially a means of removing any doubts which may arise concerning the protection of the design by the laws governing copyrights and design rights. The rules of ownership and the rights conferred are similar to those for design rights. The rights continue for 25 years provided that registration is renewed at five year intervals, but are again subject to public interest conditions.

(The Registered Designs Act 1949, as amended by The Copyrights, Designs and Patents Act 1988)

H STATE ENTERPRISES AND PUBLIC UTILITIES

European Union Law

The conduct of governments towards state enterprises and public utilities is regulated under the Treaty of Rome as follows:

> In the case of public undertakings and undertakings to which member states grant special or exclusive rights, member states shall neither enact nor maintain in force any measure contrary to the rules contained in this Treaty, in particular those provided for in . . . Articles 85 to 94.
>
> **(Article 90(1))**

and:

> Member states shall progressively adjust any state monopolies of a commercial character so as to ensure that when the transitional period has ended no discrimination regarding the conditions under which goods are procured and marketed exists between nationals of member states. The provisions of this Article shall apply to any body through which a member state in law or in fact, either directly or indirectly supervises, determines or appreciably influences imports

or exports between member states. These provisions shall likewise apply to monopolies delegated by the state to others.

(Article 37(1))

The conduct of such undertakings is regulated as follows:

Undertakings entrusted with the operation of services of general economic interest or having the character of a revenue-producing monopoly shall be subject to the rules contained in this Treaty, in particular to the rules on competition, in so far as the application of such rules does not obstruct the performance, in law or in fact of the particular tasks assigned to them. The development of trade must not be affected to such an extent as would be contrary to the interests of the Community.

(Article 90(2))

United Kingdom Law

Public Sector References
References may be made by the Secretary of State to the Monopolies and Mergers Commission concerning:

(a) the efficiency and costs of,
(b) the service provided by, or
(c) possible abuse of a monopoly situation by,

any body corporate which supplies goods or services by way of business, whose controlling members are appointed by a minister. In practice this covers most nationalised industries.

(Section 11 CA)

If the Commission finds that the public sector body in question is pursuing a course of conduct which is against the public interest, the responsible minister is empowered to order appropriate remedies.

Other Public Utilities
The regulatory authorities for the telecommunications and gas industries and for the larger privately owned airports may make references to the Monopolies and Mergers Commission under the provisions of the Telecommunications Act 1984, the Gas Act 1986, the Water In-

dustry Act 1991, the Electricity Act 1989 and the Airports Act 1986. The Commission is required to report on whether any matter operates or may be expected to operate against the public interest. An adverse finding may lead to action by the appropriate regulatory authority to remedy the adverse effects which have been found.

3 Regulatory Institutions and Procedures

A INTRODUCTION

As the previous chapter has shown, the definitions of business practices which appear in EU and United Kingdom legislation are often framed in very general terms. Application of that legislation to individual cases consequently requires the exercise of discretion going far beyond that normally required of ordinary courts of law. The legislation accordingly made provision for the creation of special institutions which were given the duty to exercise such discretion within prescribed limits and according to stated procedures. Since the legislation was first introduced, those regulatory institutions have developed further procedures and practices of their own, and have at times assumed roles which were not specifically catered for in the legislation. This chapter concentrates upon those aspects of law and practice which appear significantly to affect the conduct of the business of the regulatory authorities.

The various regulatory authorities differ in the extent to which they are involved in policy-making, as distinct from the narrower function of deciding individual cases. Policy-making in this context is taken to include both the formulation of rules and guidelines, and the use of individual cases to influence general business conduct. The EU authorities have established that decisions in particular cases may be used to deter others from further occurrences of the practices in question. There is no clear indication to that effect in United Kingdom law. Its regulatory bodies may therefore choose either to base each judgement solely upon the direct consequences of the practice before them, or to give weight also to the longer-term consequences of practices of that type. Such a dilemma could, for example, arise where the direct consequences of a merger for the public interest are finely balanced, but where that merger contributes to an upward trend in the growth of market power in an already concentrated industry. Differing approaches to that dilemma will become apparent from the analysis of cases in Part II. In some cases there are signs of a consistent and coordinated pursuit of established policy goals, and in others it would seem that policy considerations intrude only sporadically into the decision-making process.

The differing constitutions of the various regulatory bodies might be expected to influence their attitudes to policy issues. A 'collegiate' institution, governed by a body of people whose composition changes slowly might, for example, be expected to be less prone to sudden shifts of policy than would an organisation which is governed by a single appointee with a limited term of office. Similarly, the more remote the regulatory body is from day-to-day political control, the less likely are its decisions to be influenced by transitory political considerations.

For constitutional reasons, however, some degree of external control over the regulatory authorities has normally been considered necessary to guard against possible abuse of their delegated powers. In principle, one such safeguard is a power of veto by the legislature or by ministers. Another is a provision for appeal to a court of law. The possibility of appeal to a special court on matters of substance can be a source of delay, but it makes for consistency of decisions and openness in presenting the reasons for them.

A dominant influence upon the conduct of the regulatory bodies is, however, the quantity and quality of the human resources at their disposal. Those bodies are, as will be seen, very small compared with the typical organisation which they are required to regulate, and the rewards and career prospects which they offer are also generally inferior. Resource constraints thus tend to limit the extent to which initiatives are taken by the regulatory authorities, and to determine their responses to the demands made upon them. One consequence is that the majority of their work is performed informally and confidentially, using methods and procedures which are not open to review by the courts or to examination by the public. Another is that, under pressure of work, their procedures and analytical methods may sometimes be abbreviated or performed summarily.

B   EUROPEAN UNION INSTITUTIONS AND PROCEDURES

Jurisdiction

The competition rules and policies of the EU apply throughout the European Economic Area, but the institutions and procedures described below apply only where trade with members of the EU is likely to be affected, and jurisdiction over mergers is further limited by the criteria set out in section B of Chapter 6. In accordance with Article 9(3) of Regulation 17, the national authorities of member states can, if they wish, apply the prohibitions laid down in Articles 85 & 86 in their national courts, and this provision has been implemented in some EU countries, but not in Britain. Individuals in member countries may also apply to their national courts for judgements under Articles 85 and 86. In practice, however, little use has been made of the national courts for that purpose, and the implementation of EU competition law has fallen almost entirely to the European Commission and the European Courts of Justice.

The Commission

The European Commission was given a central role in competition policy by Article 89 of the Treaty of Rome:

> the Commission shall . . . ensure the application of the principles laid down in Articles 85 and 86. On application by a member state or on its own initiative, and in cooperation with the competent authorities in the member states, who shall give it their assistance, the Commission shall investigate cases of suspected infringement of these principles. If it finds that there has been an infringement, it shall propose appropriate measures to bring it to an end. If the infringement is not brought to an end, the commission shall record such an infringement in a reasoned decision. The Commission may publish its decision and authorise member states to take the measures, the conditions and details of which it shall determine, needed to remedy the situation.

The Commission consists of 17 members, nominated by member governments and supported by a permanent staff of about ten thousand. It is responsible for executing the decisions of the Council of the European Communities (see below) but is otherwise independent of the Council. In other policy areas, the Commission proposes legislative measures for enactment by the Council, but in the sphere of competition policy, it takes legally binding decisions without reference to the Council.

The Commission is supported by a Secretariat-General and by the Legal Service, which reports directly to the President of the Commission. The Legal Service advises on the legality of Commission decisions, and represents the Commission in the Court of Justice. The executive work of the Commission is done by some 20 Directorates-General, each of which is the special responsibility of one of the Commissioners.

The Directorate-General for Competition (DGIV) is divided into six Directorates:

- A – General questions of competition and coordination;
- B, C & D – Concerted practices and abuse of a dominant position (the different directorates being responsible for different groups of industries); and,
- E – State aids.
- The Mergers Task Force

DGIV is staffed by about 200 professionally qualified officials of Grade A rank including six directors and 23 divisional heads. Each division within directorates B, C and D monitors one group of industrial sectors and deals with cases affecting that group. Case officers or *rapporteurs* take responsibility for individual cases, for which they undertake economic and legal analyses, draft decisions and monitor compliance.

Other European Union Institutions

The remainder of this section of Chapter 3 is concerned mainly with the activities of the Commission, but it is first necessary to refer briefly to the relevant functions of the other Community institutions which have duties relating to competition policy. They are:

(a) The Council of the European Union
(Referred to elsewhere as 'the Council' but not to be confused with the European Council, which is a meeting of Community heads of state, nor with the Council of Europe, which is a non-community institution.)
The Council consists of one representative from the government of each member state. Under Article 87 of the Treaty, the Council has the power, acting by a qualified majority, and after consulting the European Parliament, to adopt appropriate regulations or directives proposed by the Commission to give effect to the principles set out in Articles 85 and 86 of the Treaty.
(b) The European Parliament
The Parliament, whose members are directly elected every five years, has powers to guide and supervise the Commission. It

makes an annual appraisal of the Commission's competition policy activities, expressed in the form of a resolution on the Commission's report on competition policy, and advises the Council on the Commission's legislative proposals. Similar functions are also performed by the separate Economic and Social Committee.

(c) The Court of First Instance

The Court consists of twelve members, any one of which may be called upon to act in a specific case as an advocate-general. It has jurisdiction in actions brought against the Commission or the Council on the grounds of lack of competence, infringement of an essential procedural requirement, infringement of the Treaty or of its rules of application, or misuse of powers. The Court also has the power to review and alter penalties imposed by the Commission. The Court rules only on legally binding decisions, and does not normally consider procedural irregularities unless they could effect such decisions.

It is the duty of the Court in such cases to enforce the requirement of Article 190 of the Treaty that all decisions must be reasoned. In appeals against a decision of the Commission that there has been an infringement of the Treaty, the burden of proof lies with the Commission. Thus, although in principle the Court is concerned with matters of procedure rather than of substance, it may annul a Commission decision on the grounds of error of material fact, inadequacy of reasoning or lack of adequate proof. In practice, therefore, it does become involved in the analytical merits of the Commission's arguments on matters of substance.

(d) The Court of Justice of the European Union

The Court of Justice consists of thirteen judges assisted by six Advocates-General. It hears appeals against decision of the Court of First Instance. The Court may also give preliminary rulings on matters raised in the courts of member states which bear upon the interpretation of the Treaty, or of Community legislation, or upon the validity of decisions of the Commission or of the Council. A national court may apply for such a ruling where it appears necessary to enable it to give judgement. Where such a question is raised in a case before a national court, against whose decisions there is no remedy under national law (i.e., if it is a court of final appeal), that court is required to refer the matter to the Court of Justice.

The Court's procedure normally consists of the examination

of written evidence, followed by a brief oral hearing. There is no provision for dissenting judgements.

(e) & (f) The Advisory Committee for Restrictive Practices and Monopolies and the Advisory Committee for Concentrations.

These committees comprise experts appointed by each of the member states. The appropriate committee is consulted by DGIV before referring a proposed decision to the Commission.

Notification and Clearance under Articles 85 and 86 of the Treaty

Articles 85 and 86 of the Treaty could be interpreted to prohibit any of a very wide range of business practices, many of which might alternatively be regarded as harmless. The most important function of the Commission is therefore to let businessmen know how to conform with community legislation.

Regulations are issued from time to time, conferring conditional exemption on defined groups of practices, as noted in section B of Chapter 2. Such 'block exemptions' are for a limited duration, and the regulations enable the Commission to withdraw the exemption from any particular agreement to which it takes exception. Compliance with a block exemption from Article 85(1) does not necessarily confer immunity to Article 86 (*Tetra Pak* 1990). More recent regulations also provide for an 'opposition procedure', under which certain agreements which do not automatically qualify for exemption may be notified to the Commission, and will then be considered exempt if the Commission does not take exception to them within a stated period.

Advisory notices on particular topics are also issued from time to time, and much of the Commission's work is done informally in response to requests for advice. It is probable that a major consequence of the Commission's advisory activities has been the modification or abandonment of practices which might otherwise have attracted prohibitions and penalties. Advice obtained in that way is not, however, binding upon the Commission. To obtain legal immunity from prohibitions and penalties for practices not covered by block exemptions, it is necessary to follow the formal procedures of *notification and application for negative clearance*.

Notification is a procedure by which an agreement falling within Article 85(1) of the Treaty can be exempted under the provisions of Article 85(3) (see Section B of Chapter 2, above). However, under Article 4(2) of Regulation 17, notification of an agreement is not necessary for that purpose in the case of agreements within one member state which do not affect trade between member states. There is no legal requirement to notify an agreement, but notification confers interim immunity from penalties, and enables the agreement to be given retrospective legal validity if exemption is obtained. With the exceptions noted above, it is the only means by which exemption can be obtained.

Application for negative clearance is a procedure for seeking a declaration that a practice falls outside the scope of Article 85(1) and/or Article 86 of the Treaty. It is normal practice to submit such an application at the same time as a notification, and on the same form (Form A/B). Unlike notification, application does not confer interim immunity from penalties.

On receipt of a notification or application, the Commission may seek further information from applicants or from third parties, and may suggest amendments to the arrangements that may make them acceptable. If, after examination, the Commission intends to grant the application, it must publish a summary and invite comments from third parties. It must also consult the Advisory Committee on Restrictive Practices. An agreement for which a formal exemption is granted remains legally valid for the period of the exemption and a negative clearance remains in legal force unless or until it is revised in the light of a change in circumstances.

As an alternative to granting formal exemption or negative clearance, the Commission may send the parties a *comfort letter* indicating that it has closed its file on the matter, because it sees no need to take any further action. Most applications and notifications are in fact dealt with in this way. In some cases, the Commission first publishes a summary and invites comments, as it does before making a formal decision. A comfort letter is not legally binding on the Commission, but it is likely to have a strong effect on any subsequent decision on the matter. A comfort letter can sometimes be obtained in a matter of months, as compared with periods of 18 months, or often much longer, in the case of a formal decision. Where it sees obstacles to the granting of negative clearance the Commission may issue a *warning letter*, explaining its concerns and giving companies the opportunity to offer undertakings or to present a defence.

Notification and Clearance of Mergers

Every qualifying merger must be notified to the Commission by the acquirer, if it is to be an acquisition; or otherwise jointly by the merging parties. Regulation 3384/94 stipulates the form of notification to be used. Notification of a merger is linked to its automatic suspension for an initial period of three weeks. The Commission may extend that suspension by order, but must decide within one month whether to initiate proceedings. If proceedings are initiated, a decision must be taken within a further four months, during which period the parties may propose changes to the merger with a view to gaining its clearance. The Commission may, under some circumstances, refer a case to the competition authorities of a member state (as noted in Section B of Chapter 6).

The Commission's Powers of Investigation

Something like 90 per cent of cases dealt with by the Commission are in response to applications and notifications, and the bulk of those cases are settled informally. The Commission also has a (rarely used) power under Article 12 of Regulation 17 to conduct a general inquiry into any economic sector in which it believes that competition is being restricted or distorted within the Common Market. The remaining cases arise from the investigation of complaints and from initiatives taken as a result of the Commission's own monitoring activities.

Requests for information for the purposes of such inquiries follow the two-stage procedure laid down in Article 11 of Regulation 17:

(a) a written request for information, stating the purpose of the inquiry and its legal basis, which is copied to the Office of Fair Trading;

(b) if the required information is not fully supplied within the stated time limit, a further request based upon a formal Commission decision, stipulating in detail what information is required.

Failure to supply all of the information requested may then attract a fine and a daily penalty.

Powers to enter premises and examine business records are also provided by Article 14 of Regulation 17. A Commission official may demand entry – if necessary without warning – on production of a written authorisation indicating the purpose and subject matter of the investigation. He is normally accompanied by an official of the Office of Fair Trading. There is no right of forcible entry, but the Commission may if necessary obtain an order from the High Court requiring admission. Business records may be copied but not removed, and oral explanations may be asked for. The procedures governing the disclosure of confidential information provided to the Commission are described in Annex 3.1 below.

Formal Procedures

If the results of an investigation indicate that there has been a breach of the competition rules, the DGIV will usually try to put an end to that breach by meetings or correspondence with those concerned. Alternatively, or if that fails, the following procedure is adopted in full:

(a) a formal *Statement of Objections*, briefly setting out the relevant facts, the supporting evidence and the proposed legal findings, is sent to the parties concerned, together with copies of other relevant documents;

(b) the parties concerned are usually given restricted access to the relevant Commission files to enable them to make use of other documents in their defence;

(c) the parties concerned, and other interested parties, may make written submissions within a stipulated time limit;

(d) at the request of the parties concerned or of other interested parties, there may be an oral hearing, as described below;

(e) DGIV consults the Advisory Committee on Restrictive Practices: (or, in merger cases, the Advisory Committee on Concentrations)

(f) The competition commissioner makes a recommendation to his fellow commissioners, and the Commission makes and publishes its decision.

Hearings are organised and chaired by the *Hearing Officer* whose duty it is to protect the rights of the defence. (The Hearing Officer reports to the Director-General for Competition but has direct access to the Commissioner responsible for competition. His full terms of reference are set out in Commission Decision of 23 November 1990 – and are described in Comp Rep 23 (1993) par 203.) Apart from the representatives of the parties concerned, those attending may include representatives of member states and other interested parties. Proceedings are opened by a brief statement by a Commission official. The parties then make their presentations, and other witnesses may be heard. The parties may then be questioned by representatives of the Commission or of member states. Minutes are kept and must be agreed by those heard. The procedure throughout is intended to be administrative rather than adversarial or judicial. Hearings are held in private and do not usually last more than a day. Formal mergers procedures are generally similar, but their operation is governed by strict time limits. The required procedures and time limits are set out in Commission regulations 2367/90 and 3384/94.

Remedies and Penalties

Infringements which are revealed by the above procedures are often remedied by voluntary action by the parties concerned. Remedies which may be ordered by the Commission include:

(a) an order to terminate an agreement or practice;
(b) an order to take positive action (for instance, to resume supplies which have been withheld);
(c) an order requiring a company to divest itself of a company which it had acquired.

The power of the Commission to regulate prices which are considered to be excessive has not yet been determined.

The Commission is also empowered to impose fines and periodic penalty payments on undertakings which intentionally or negligently infringe Article 85(1) or Article 86 of the Treaty. Infringements which lead to the imposition of fines are not regarded as criminal offences, but it has been established that they may be used as a general deterrent to other undertakings. Fines may range from one thousand to a maximum of one million ECU or 10 per cent of turnover, whichever is the greater.

General Comments

In principle, the Commission has extensive powers to formulate policy, propose legislation, investigate suspected infringements, enforce remedies and punish offenders. In practice, it has the resources for only a limited formal exercise of those powers. The number of cases on which it makes formal decisions averages about a dozen a year.

The formal rules and procedures which have been described above are consequently of less importance than the informal advice which has been given by officials of the Commission. The nature of that advice, and the position under British law of those who rely upon it, must for the time being remain a matter of some uncertainty.

C THE OFFICE OF FAIR TRADING

The Duties of the Director-General

The Director-General of Fair Trading occupies a focal position in competition policy in Britain. His duties under the Treaty of Rome, the Fair Trading Act 1973, the Restrictive Trade Practices Act 1976, the Competition Act 1980 and the Financial Services Act 1986 may be summarised as follows:

(a) to act (jointly with the Department of Trade and Industry) as *United Kingdom Competent Authority* under the Treaty, with representation on the Advisory Committee on Restrictive Practices and Monopolies, and the Advisory Committee on Concentrations and with the duties to assist the Commission which have been referred to above;

(b) *to collect and collate information* concerning commercial activities in the United Kingdom and to monitor possible monopoly or merger situations or uncompetitive practices which may adversely affect the economic interests of consumers; and to advise the Secretary of State for Trade and Industry concerning appropriate remedial action;

(c) in particular, to advise the Secretary of State whether to make a *merger reference* to the Monopolies and Mergers Commission;

(d) where he thinks fit, to make a *monopoly reference* to the Monopolies and Mergers Commission;

(e) to initiate and carry out investigations to establish whether an *anti-competitive practice* is being pursued; if it is, to seek appropriate undertakings from those pursuing it; and if satisfactory undertakings are not received, and he thinks it appropriate to do so, to make a *competition reference* to the Monopolies and Mergers Commission;

(f) to advise the Secretary of State concerning the feasibility of remedies proposed by the Monopolies and Mergers Commission;

(g) at the request of the Secretary of State, and where the Monopolies and Mergers Commission have made an adverse public interest finding, to *seek understakings* from those concerned and to monitor the carrying out of such undertakings, or to monitor compliance with orders made by the Secretary of State;

(h) to compile and maintain a register of registrable *restrictive trade practices*, and to take proceedings on them before the Restrictive

Trade Practices Court (with exceptions established under the procedures described below); and,

(i) to examine the rules of the regulatory agencies set up under the Financial Services Act and to report to the Secretary of State concerning their effects on competition.

The Director-General is given no special duties by the Resale Prices Act 1976, but Section 34 of the Fair Trading Act requires him to seek assurances of good behaviour from those whom he believes to have breached its provisions, and if necessary to bring proceedings against them before the Restrictive Practices Court.

The Director-General also has extensive statutory duties in the field of consumer protection, including duties in connection with the codes of practice of trade associations.

Until the passing of the Deregulation and Contracting Out Act 1994, the Director-General was largely dependent upon complaints and announcements in the press for the information necessary to enable him to decide whether to initiate formal action. As from 1995, however, the Director-General can require a firm to provide any information necessary to enable him to decide whether to make a reference to the Monopolies and Mergers Commission under the Competition Act, and there are penalties for noncompliance. It is anticipated that the existence of that power will encourage firms to cooperate in providing the information necessary to undertake his other duties (Howe, 1994).

The Independence of the Director-General

The Director-General is appointed by the Secretary of State for Trade and Industry but he enjoys a considerable degree of independence. The Secretary of State has the power to prevent him from making competition investigations and monopoly references, and also to give him general directions concerning the conduct of his duties, but those powers can only be exercised publicly, and in practice they have seldom been used. As already noted, the Secretary of State can exempt an agreement from registration under the Restrictive Trade Practices Act but he can do so only on or before the conclusion of the agreement, after which he has no powers to intervene – except, of course, by special legislation. In the exceptional case of the proceedings taken by the Director-General against restrictive trade practices in the Stock Exchange, an Act of Parliament was passed in 1983 to exempt the Stock Exchange in return for the abandonment of certain of its restrictions.

The Secretary of State is free to ignore the Director-General's advice concerning merger references, and the legislation does not require him to reveal what advice he has been given, nor to give reasons for rejecting it. The Director-General's advice to refer has been overruled 13 times and his advice not to refer has been overruled 6 times.

As regards individual cases, the Director-General thus enjoys almost total independence, but he cannot act independently on matters of competition policy. Although he has a strong influence upon the development of policy in his role as adviser to the Secretary of State, the final decisions on policy matters inevitably rest with the Secretary of State. The Director-General is not a civil servant, but on matters of general policy his standing is similar to that of a Permanent Secretary. He is bound to give effect to any publicly announced changes of government policy, and it must be assumed that he also takes account of unpublished expressions of the Secretary of State's wishes. An awareness of government policy also influences decisions and recommendations concerning references to the Monopolies and Mergers Commission. A former Director-General has explained that

> if I did not follow broadly the declared Government policy there would be, or there might be, a great deal of difference of view and businessmen would not know quite where they were. (Borrie, 1991)

The Resources of the Office of Fair Trading

The Director-General has observed that the resources available to him are severely limited, that consequently he has to make difficult choices, and that he cannot be expected to pursue every complaint made to him about the behaviour of firms (DGFT, 1981). Within staffing limits imposed by the Civil Service Department, he is empowered to recruit his own staff and to delegate to them any of his competition policy powers. He is supported by a Deputy Director-General. (Civil Service Grade 2 – formerly Deputy Secretary) and a permanent staff of around four hundred, including 16 professional economists, two professional accountants and 12 lawyers. The majority of his staff are, however, engaged upon work in connection with consumer protection. Only about a hundred of them are concerned with competition policy, reporting through four Assistant Directors (Civil Service Grade 5) to the Director of Competition Policy (Civil Service Grade 3 – formerly Under Secretary). With occasional exceptions, the more senior staff of the Office of Fair Trading are career civil servants on secondment from government departments.

The Conduct of the Business of the Office of Fair Trading

Within the framework outlined above, the legislation leaves the Director-General free to decide his own procedures. With the exception of investigations undertaken under the Competition Act, formal procedures are, however, of comparatively small importance in the work of the Competition Policy Division because its resources are devoted mainly to monitoring, following up complaints, and giving informal advice to businessmen or persuading them to alter their behaviour.

Notwithstanding what has been said about the limitations upon the resources available to the Director-General, and upon his powers to demand information, his officials can be extremely effective in dealing informally with those cases which come to their attention. They are greatly assisted in that respect by the uncertainty which many businessmen experience concerning the risks of becoming involved in the protracted and costly procedures of the Restrictive Trade Practices Court or of the Monopolies and Mergers Commission. Advice on how to remain on the safe side of such risks is normally followed, and the advice given is probably somewhat more cautious than could strictly be justified by the legislation or by precedent.

Thus, although the legislation does not formally empower the Director-General to make judgements concerning the public interest nor to enforce particular standards of behaviour among businessmen, he and his officials do in practice exert and enforce such judgements. (In principle, the Director-General does not allow his judgement of the merits of a case to influence his decision whether it should go to the Court or to the Commission. That decision is determined by his assessment of the importance of the case – with the possible qualification that there would be no point in referring a case which offered no prospect of a remedy.) Their informal influence upon business behaviour is consequently far greater than the influence of the formal procedures of the other regulatory institutions. In the last resort, however, that influence derives from the power to resort to those formal procedures. Thus the interpretation of the public interest which the Director-General and his officials employ cannot be entirely their own, but must ultimately be influenced by their perception of the interpretation likely to be put upon it by the Commission or the Court.

Procedures

The procedures underlying the more formal functions of the Office of Fair Trading may be summarised as follows.

Monopoly and Competition Act References
When the Director-General considers there to be a case for making a reference to the Monopolies and Mergers Commission, the procedure adopted is broadly as follows:

- (a) the firm is informed of the reasons for a possible reference and is asked to supply relevant information;
- (b) if it is decided to proceed, the firm is invited to offer enforceable undertakings as an alternative to a reference to the Monopolies and Mergers Commission;
- (c) the Director-General discusses any proposed undertakings, and possible amendments thereto, with the firms concerned and with any other interested parties;
- (d) if undertakings emerge which are considered by the Director-General to be acceptable, they are published together with the reasons for considering that they would remedy otherwise adverse effects on the public interest, and third-party comments are invited;
- (e) if no undertakings are offered or if the Director-General decides not to accept the proferred undertakings (or, in the case of a Monopoly reference, recommend their acceptance by the Secretary of State) then he may make a reference to the Commission.

Under the two-stage Competition Act procedure then operating, 35 preliminary investigations were undertaken by the Office of Fair Trading, as a result of which 10 references were made to the Monopolies and Mergers Commission during the period 1980–93; a further 10 were settled by undertakings to the Director-General; and in the remainder, no uncompetitive practices were found. The Director-General made 54 monopoly references during the period 1979–93. The number of monopoly and competition references has thus averaged about four a year, and before the introduction of enforceable undertakings in 1995, some two or three cases a year were being dealt with by informal and unenforceable undertakings to the Office of Fair Trading.

Merger References
The procedure for deciding whether to recommend the reference of a merger is dominated by the need for speed and secrecy. If a merger seems to come within the scope of the legislation, the Office may ask the parties for further information and in some cases either the Office or the parties may ask for a meeting. A paper prepared from available information, including the parties' submissions, is then despatched to

members of the Mergers Panel (which consists of nominees of selected government departments). In contentious cases, or if a reference is likely, a meeting of the Panel is called at which Office officials present an analysis, departmental officials put forward ministerial or departmental views, and the Director-General makes his decision. The recommendation which goes to the Secretary of State is in any case that of the Director-General alone.

Requests for confidential advice on proposed mergers are evaluated by the Office in the same way as published cases except that the Office cannot consult more widely, and so is dependent upon published information or information supplied by the applicants. The Director-General advises the Secretary of State in the normal way and seeks his authorisation to inform the parties whether the proposal is likely to be referred.

The Companies Act 1989 introduced a voluntary pre-notification procedure whose aim is to provide accelerated clearance for straightforward cases which raise no competition or other public interest issues. The Act also allows the Secretary of State to accept undertakings on divestment from parties to a merger instead of referring the merger to the Commission, and the Deregulation and Contracting Out Act 1994 extended this to other types of undertaking, such as undertakings concerning behaviour.

Merger activity fluctuates greatly from year to year, but on average some 2–300 cases a year have been examined, of which confidential guidance has been given for about 40 and about 10 (3 per cent) have been referred to the Commission.

Restrictive Trade Practices

When an agreement has been submitted to the office for registration, the procedure adopted is as follows:

(a) the information is examined for the completeness of the relevant facts and further information is sought where necessary, and if, after analysing the often complex legal issues involved, the agreement is considered not to be registrable, all documents are then returned; otherwise it is entered in the Register;

(b) the registered agreement is then examined to decide whether it contains restrictions which are of sufficient significance to warrant investigation by the Restrictive Practices Court, and there are usually discussions with the parties to the agreement with a view to modifying it so that it does not;

(c) where the remaining restrictions are not then considered of sufficient significance, an application is made to the Secretary of State for Trade and Industry for a direction under Section 21(2) of the Act, discharging the Director-General from his duty to take proceedings in the Court;

(d) otherwise, agreements which have not in the meantime been abandoned are then brought before the Court (unless the Director-General decides otherwise in view of decisions taken by the European Commission);

(e) if there is a breach of an order of the Court or a breach of any undertaking given to the Court, the Director-General may take legal action for contempt of court against the firms concerned or their directors.

(For a more detailed account of the above procedures, see Green 1986.)

The result of adopting form-based criteria for registration is that very large numbers of agreements are registrable, many of which have no anti-competitive effects. 581 agreements were added to the register in 1994, bringing the total since the register was established in 1956 to just under 12,000.

The remaining procedure is dominated nowadays by stages (b) and (c) above, in which the negotiated 'filleting' of agreements to remove restrictive clauses is often followed by directions under Section 21(2). In 1994, over 1200 agreements were cleared by that procedure. The time taken for stages (a) to (c) is typically around two years. If 'filleting' negotiations are unsuccessful and the case goes to court, the process may take over three years. Since 1980, however, the Court has been used almost entirely to process undefended cases – which is done in order to bring them within (e) above.

General Comments

The delegation of extensive regulatory powers to a single person was, at the time of the Fair Trading Act, constitutionally unusual; collegiate-style bodies had hitherto been the norm. As safeguards, he was not given the formal power to make judgements concerning the public interest, and the exercise of his powers was made subject to a degree of ministerial oversight. In addition, the Director-General's actions are subject to judicial review as noted in section G below. In practice, those safeguards have seldom imposed any serious limitations upon the day-to-day exercise of his duties. What the Office of Fair Trading

has been able to do has been governed mainly by its limited powers of
investigation, and by resource constraints. For information concerning
the existence of anti-competitive practices it must rely mainly upon
complaints – of which its Competition Division handles nearly a thousand a year. With a staff of only about a hundred, who have other
time-consuming duties to perform, it must be highly selective in following up even the most convincing of those complaints; and only a
minute proportion of them lead to any reported action. Its effectiveness in regulating business behaviour depends mainly upon the informal exercise of its powers of persuasion; and those powers of persuasion
depend to a large extent upon the fear on the part of businessmen of
being involved in expensive and protracted procedures, the outcome
of which is hard to predict.

The Director-General has said that:

> It has always been a basic tenet of my Office that it is an open
> organisation, willing at all times to communicate and to listen . . .
> people in trade and industry should know that they are always wel-
> come to discuss matters with me or my staff. (DGFT 1979)

The giving of confidential advice has been the Office's main method
of communication, but – apart from its generally informative annual
reports – it has been less forthcoming in its published statements.
Guidebooks are available concerning the conduct of the various functions of the Office, but they do not go far beyond explaining in simple
terms the formal rules and procedures which are laid down in the relevant legislation. Little or no published guidance is available to indicate more specifically the treatment which is accorded to particular
business practices. The basis on which the Office conducts the vast
majority of its business is thus hidden from public view.

D THE MONOPOLIES AND MERGERS COMMISSION

Duties

Duties are assigned to the Monopolies and Mergers Commission under
the Fair Trading Act 1973, under the Competition Act 1980 and under
subsequent privatisation acts. The Commission has to inquire into the
facts of the cases specifically referred to it, to identify situations or
actions in those cases which it judges to be against the public interest,

and, where appropriate, to recommend remedies. The Commission has no role in the selection of its cases nor in following up the results of its inquiries. Unlike the Office of Fair Trading, it does not monitor the behaviour of businessmen before or after a formal inquiry.

Inquiries may be called for by any of seven types of reference:

(a) *general references* under S78 of the Fair Trading Act (see section D of Chapter 2);

(b) *competition references* under S6 of the Competition Act (see section D of Chapter 2) following an investigation of possible anti-competitive practices by the Office of Fair Trading (see section C of this chapter);

(c) *merger references* under SS57–77 of the Fair Trading Act (see section F of Chapter 2) – including newspaper mergers (not dealt with in this book);

(d) *monopoly references* under SS47–56 of the Fair Trading Act (see section C of Chapter 2);

(e) *restrictive labour practice references* under S79 of the Fair Trading Act (see section E of Chapter 2);

(f) *public sector references* under S11 of the Competition Act (see section H of Chapter 2);

(g) *gas, telecommunication, electricity, water, broadcasting and airport references* under the various privatisation Acts (see section H of Chapter 2).

In monopoly inquiries, general inquiries and inquiries under the privatisation acts, the Commission's statutory duties specifically exclude the consideration of registrable restrictive practices or of resale price maintenance, but it can be required to inquire into matters involving any other aspect of national competition law.

In its reports on merger, monopoly and restrictive labour practice references, the Commission is required to come to definite conclusions as to:

(a) whether the specified situation or practice exists; and if so,

(b) whether anything arising from it operates, or may be expected to operate against the public interest (except for monopoly references confined to the facts); and if so,

(c) what particular effects, adverse to the public interest it has or may be expected to have.

Conclusion (a) is not required for general references because in those cases the existence of the situation or practice is not at issue.

In reporting its conclusions, the Commission is required to include an account of the reasons for them, and – to the extent that it considers it expedient for a proper understanding of those conclusions – a survey of the general position covered by the reference and of the developments leading up to it. Where adverse effects are found, the report may also recommend remedies. Reports are made to the Secretary of State, who responds to them as described in section F of this chapter.

Composition and Structure

The Commission has a dual structure with a formal division of functions between *members* and *staff*. Members are appointed by the Secretary of State for Trade and Industry and are responsible for the contents of the reports made to him. The staff are appointed by the Commission and their functions are to collect and analyse information, to prepare drafts of the Commission's reports and to give advice. Formally speaking, the term 'the Commission' is taken to refer collectively to all of its members, but the report of each inquiry is the responsibility solely of those members who are engaged on it, and individual members among them are free to express dissenting views.

Members are appointed for their ability and experience, and not as representatives of particular interests. (In 1995 they numbered 31 including four lawyers, five professional economists and one professional accountant. Some 16 of them were or had been company directors, and one of them had been a senior trade union official.) Members are appointed for a renewable three-year term, and the average member has served on the Commission for about five years. The Chairman is appointed on a full-time basis and the other members are appointed to devote an average of one and a half days a week to the Commission's business. Three of them are appointed Deputy Chairmen. For newspaper mergers and telecommunications references, additional members are appointed to an inquiry from panels maintained by the Secretary of State of people with special experience in those fields.

The staff number about 85, headed by the Secretary to the Commission (Civil Service Grade 3 – formerly Under-Secretary). It is organised into three specialist divisions – containing, respectively, accountants, economists and industrial advisers – and five administrative divisions.

There are also full-time legal advisers. About half the staff are civil servants on secondment from government departments, and the remainder are direct employees of the Commission or businessmen on secondment.

Powers

The Commission has powers to require any person to attend to give evidence or to produce any documents relevant to an inquiry, and to require information from any person carrying on a business (broadly, such as he could be compelled to produce in civil proceedings before a court). It has not so far found it necessary to use those statutory powers. Procedures concerning the disclosure of confidential information provided to the Commission are outlined in Annex 3.1 below.

Procedures

The legislation leaves the Commission free to determine its own procedures subject to general directions by the Secretary of State. However, time limits have come to have a major influence upon methods of working. (The report of an inquiry is legally void if it is not delivered within a statutory time limit or beyond the time limit stipulated in the reference unless an extension has previously been applied for and granted by the Secretary of State.) There is no statutory time limit on monopoly inquiries: in the past a period of two years was normal, but this has recently been substantially reduced, sometimes to as short as nine months. Merger and competition references are statutorily limited to a maximum of six months, with provision for an extension of up to a further three months, but nowadays the time limit normally specified for merger references is three months. Inquiries under the Telecommunications, Gas and Airport Acts are also limited to a maximum of six months, but there are provisions for extensions of up to a further six months. In most cases these statutory time limits have recently been supplemented by very much shorter target timetables.

Procedures differ in a number of other respects as between different types of reference, but their principal common features are broadly as follows.

Preliminaries

(a) It has been the practice for a group of not less than five members to be appointed by the Chairman to conduct an inquiry –

then referred to throughout that inquiry as 'the Group' – chaired (usually) by himself or one of the Deputy Chairmen. However, the minimum size of a group was, for most types of inquiry, reduced to three in January 1989, so somewhat smaller groups may now be used from time to time, particularly for the smaller mergers. A team of officials is brought together to support the Group throughout the inquiry, including a Team Manager, a Reference Secretary and selected staff from the specialist divisions.

(b) The Reference Secretary circulates a background paper summarising available information, together with a draft work programme and timetable for the main stages of the inquiry. This has to be strictly tailored to the time limit stipulated in the reference.

Fact-finding

(c) In monopoly or merger inquiries, it is first necessary to establish that a statutory monopoly or merger situation exists. Written submissions are invited from parties concerned and from other interested parties. In merger inquiries the main parties are then asked to make written submissions of their case for the merger – or against it when it is contested. In monopoly inquiries, and in some other types of inquiry, questionnaires and requests for documents are sent to those concerned – designed to elicit factual information which might be relevant to the reference. In some cases, user surveys are also commissioned.

(d) After reviewing written responses and reporting progress to the Group, the staff – accompanied sometimes by members of the Group – may visit the respondents to seek clarification or further information. The Group as a whole may also make informal visits in order to obtain a general understanding of the background.

(e) The staff then present summaries of the information which they have obtained to the Group, drawing attention to issues which the Group might consider to be relevant to their inquiry.

Hearings

(f) The Commission may offer interested parties the opportunity to attend – or ask them to attend – preliminary hearings to clarify facts, and sometimes to discuss the issues which are relevant to the inquiry. Hearings take place in private, normally with each party appearing separately. Statements by the parties are followed by questions from members of the Group. The procedure adopted is intended to be investigatory not adversarial, but parties may be legally represented if they so wish. A verbatim record of the proceedings is made, and sent to each party for checking.

(g) After further discussions, the staff prepare and obtain the Group's approval for the issue of *Public Interest Letters* to the principal parties in the case of monopoly inquiries, or a list of issues in other cases. The Group will not at this stage have reached any conclusion concerning the public interest, and the purpose of those communications is to warn those who are to attend the main hearing of the issues about which the Group will wish to ask questions.

(h) At the main hearing, the procedure is as described in (f) above, but the public interest letter, or the list of issues is used as the agenda. The main purpose is to give those attending an opportunity to respond to any points which might be interpreted as criticisms of their behaviour or proposals. The occasion may also be taken to discuss possible remedies for any matters which might be found to be against the public interest. If necessary there may be a further hearing to discuss remedies.

Reporting

(i) Work is in the meantime in hand on drafts of the factual portion of the Group's report. The Reference Secretary draws together contributions from other members of the team, and drafts are progressively 'put back' to those who provided the information for comments on factual accuracy, and any representations concerning confidentiality. At appropriate stages, the drafts are also put to the Group for comment or approval.

(j) After the conclusion of the hearings, the Group meets to discuss proposed conclusions and recommendations, and to consider drafts of the concluding sections of their report. There are no consultations with outsiders concerning the Group's public interest conclusions.

(k) There is finally a 'settle and sign' meeting of the Group at which final amendments are made and each member signs a copy of the report, and at which those who disagree with the majority conclusion may table statements of their dissent for incorporation in the report.

Some elements of the above procedure are used for public-sector inquiries, but their conduct is different because their main focus is usually upon efficiency. General references have been infrequent, and the procedures used have been adapted to the circumstances of each inquiry.

The Role of the Commission

The Commission's reports in response to general references (on topics such as collective discrimination, parallel pricing, and full-line forcing and tie-in sales) have often had an important influence upon the development of British competition policy – besides providing businessmen with valuable indications of the Commission's attitude to such practices. Generally speaking, the Commission has not otherwise been involved in the formulation of policy. Recommendations which go beyond the terms of the reference in question have occasionally appeared in other reports, but inquiry groups have normally restricted themselves to the merits of individual cases.

The Commission's constitution and procedures do not, in any case, lend themselves to the role of a policy-making body. Decisions are made, not by the Commission as a collegiate body, but by the groups of members assigned to particular inquiries. Groups are not bound by precedent, but decide each case on its merits. Consequently, different groups have in the past occasionally taken divergent views of similar issues. In recent years an attempt has been made to improve the consistency of decision-making by means of seminars and of circulated papers, but each group remains free to reach its decisions, independently of the other members of the Commission.

The Commission's principal role arises from the fact that unless it makes an adverse public interest judgement on a case, neither the Secretary of State nor anyone else has the power to take any remedial action. In response to an adverse public interest finding, the Secretary of State is free to ignore the Commission's recommendations or to apply remedies of his own choosing, but he seldom does so. The practical significance of an adverse public interest finding thus stems mainly from the remedies which it makes possible. There have been occasions when a public interest finding has in fact been determined by a group's view of possible remedies. In its report on the wholesaling of petrol, one group found the practice of selective price support to be anticompetitive but saw serious disadvantages in regulations to prohibit that practice. They concluded that:

> On balance therefore, having regard to the likely adverse effects if it were disallowed, we conclude that selective support . . . does not operate against the public interest. (*Petrol 1979*, par 135)

In another case, however, a group made an adverse public interest finding in circumstances under which they found it inappropriate to recommend a remedy (*Tampons 1980*).

In the performance of their various roles, members of the Commission traditionally attach great importance to their independence. In particular, they do not feel in any way bound to act in accordance with the wishes of government ministers. Views submitted to the Commission by government departments are considered and published in the same way as evidence from any other interest. Departments are not consulted further when conclusions and recommendations are being considered, notwithstanding the fact that the Secretary of State is free to reject an adverse finding and to depart from the Commission's recommendations. The Commission takes great pains to adopt procedures which avoid any possibility of yielding to hidden pressures from interested parties. For example, although account may be taken of undertakings offered by the parties, the Commission does not engage in bargaining with them.

E   THE RESTRICTIVE PRACTICES COURT

(As indicated in the introduction to Chapter 1, the treatment in this book of procedures under the Restrictive Practices Act is more cursory than that of other aspects of competition practice, in view of the extensive treatment of the subject elsewhere. For a more detailed treatment, the reader is referred in particular to Green, 1986.)

Powers and Duties

The Restrictive Practices Court has jurisdiction to declare whether restrictions or information agreements referred to it by the Director-General of Fair Trading are contrary to the public interest. On application from the Director-General, the Court may make orders restraining those concerned from giving effect to such agreements or making other agreements to the like effect. The Court may also make an order exempting particular goods from the provisions of the Resale Prices Act which prohibit individually enforced resale price maintenance. The Court's powers and procedures resemble those of the High Court.

The Court is nowadays seldom used except for the formal processing of undefended cases. In its 1988 White Paper the Government was proposing to transfer the functions of the Court to the Office of Fair Trading and the Monopolies and Mergers Commission.

The Composition of the Court

The Court consists of five High Court judges and ten lay members chosen by the Lord Chancellor. Hearings are presided over by one of the judges who is generally accompanied by two lay members.

Procedures

The Court deals separately with each of the restrictions contained in an agreement. If any restriction is not defended, the Court is bound to find it to be against the public interest, and will then usually issue an order forbidding its operation.

For defended restrictions, the procedure is broadly as follows:

(a) a representative of the defendants files a *Statement of Case*, specifying the restrictive practices to which they admit, indicating which of the statutory defences they wish to plead (see Table 1 of Chapter 2) and putting forward the case that the restrictions are not unreasonable, and that their advantages outweigh any possible detriments to the public interest;

(b) the Director-General files an *Answer* to the defendants' statement, admitting or denying their contentions as to facts, specifying restrictive practices not admitted by them, and stipulating the detriments which he alleges to result;

(c) the defendants may, if they wish, file a *Reply* relating to any matters not referred to by the Director-General;

(d) the Court commences a formal *Hearing*, adopting the normal procedures of a civil court;

(e) the Court decides whether it accepts that any of the statutory defences has been successfully made, and if so whether on balance any of the restrictions concerned are not unreasonable; and only if it is satisfied on all of those points may it rule that those restrictions are not against the public interest.

Proceedings relating to defended agreements may last two years or more, although the actual hearing may only last a few days. Most of the time is taken up with the exchange of pleadings and with the accountancy and other investigations required to establish all the facts about the restrictions. The Court may, however, make an interim order forbidding the operation of a restriction if it is satisfied that it cannot reasonably be expected to satisfy one of the statutory defences and that it may cause material detriments during the course of the Court's proceedings. Unless such an order is made, the restrictions may be operated until the Court has reached a decision.

F THE SECRETARY OF STATE

The Secretary of State for Trade and Industry plays the leading role in the development of British competition policy. As the Cabinet Minister responsible for competition policy, he is responsible for placing before parliament the Government's proposals for competition legislation. He appoints the Director-General of Fair Trading and the members of the Monopolies and Mergers Commission, and may give them limited general directions concerning the conduct of their duties. He alone has the power to refer mergers to the Commission, and to determine and impose remedies following an adverse public interest finding by the Commission; and in those respects he acts as a regulatory authority in his own right.

In the exercise of his various powers the Secretary of State is responsible to Parliament, and he thus provides the link with Parliament which is the constitutional safeguard accompanying Parliament's delegation of discretionary powers to the Director-General and to the Commission. He is not, however, responsible to Parliament for their conduct of individual cases.

Formal Powers

The Secretary of State's statutory powers are:

(a) to make or revoke an order under Section 29 of the Restrictive Trade Practices Act exempting from the provisions of the Act any agreement which he considers to be of substantial importance to the national economy, and which is not already exempted under the Act;

(b) to give a direction under Section 21(2) of the Restrictive Trade Practices Act, discharging the Director-General of Fair Trading at his request from his duty to take a registered agreement to the Restrictive Practices Court, where that agreement is not of such significance to warrant investigation by the Court;

(c) to make a general reference, a merger reference, a monopoly reference, a restrictive labour practice reference or a public sector reference to the Monopolies and Mergers Commission;

(d) to direct the Director-General of Fair Trading not to proceed with the investigation of an anti-competitive practice under the Competition Act, and to direct the Monopolies and Mergers Commission not to proceed with a competition reference under that act;

(e) to give general directions to the Director-General of Fair Trading concerning considerations to which he should have particular regard in considering whether to make a monopoly reference, and to give directions concerning procedures to the Monopolies and Mergers Commission;

(f) to publish reports of the Director-General of Fair Trading and of the Monopolies and Mergers Commission, having excluded from them any matters which he considers it would be against the public interest to publish.

(g) in respect only of matters identified in a report of the Monopolies and Mergers Commission as being against the public interest, to make such orders under Schedule 8 of the Fair Trading Act as he considers necessary to remedy or prevent the adverse effects identified in the report.

Orders under Schedule 8 of the Fair Trading Act, referred to in (g) above, can declare unlawful any of a virtually unlimited range of anti-competitive practices, prohibit a merger, or order the splitting up of a business. Such orders are normally used to give legal effect to the recommendations of the Commission, but the Secretary of State does occasionally take action which is different from that recommended.

The independent power to make monopoly references, referred to in (c), is used to make references which the Director-General is debarred from making under Section 50(3) of the Fair Trading Act, and not to override the Director-General's powers. (The goods and services with which Section 50(3) is concerned include gas, electricity and water, transport and ports, postal services, some radio and television services and some agricultural products. A reference concerning one of those products is made jointly with the responsible minister.)

The power to make a merger reference has normally been exercised in accordance with the Director-General's recommendations – with occasional exceptions as noted in section C above and in Chapter 6. The Secretary of State need not give reasons for his decisions.

As noted in Annex 3.1, the Secretary of State has the power to order excisions from the reports of the Director-General and of the Commission in order to preserve commercial confidentiality.

In common with those of other ministers on whom Parliament has conferred decision-making powers, the decisions of the Secretary of State are subject to judicial review as noted in section G below.

Informal Influences

Apart from the Secretary of State's publicly exercised statutory powers, it must be assumed that he and his ministerial colleagues are able to exert some degree of informal influence upon the Director General of Fair Trading. They are, as has been noted, represented in an advisory capacity on the Mergers Panel, and it would not be surprising if their officials also made representations to him concerning other types of reference. Sponsoring departments may on occasion wish to avoid possible conflicts between departmental policies and the recommendations of the Commission, or may prefer to use the threat of a reference to persuade their industries to behave more competitively. The Director-General is free to resist such pressures and make a reference, but he may on occasion see departmental action as a more effective way of achieving his objectives. There may, on the other hand, be occasions when sponsoring departments actively seek a reference in order to put pressure on recalcitrant organisations.

Once a reference has been made, it is extremely unlikely that the Secretary of State could exert any influence upon its findings. His officials may, at the outset of an inquiry which he has referred, meet the Commission to indicate the reasons for the reference, but the Commission takes pains thereafter to avoid any contact with government in connection with the case.

On receipt of a report which contains adverse public interest findings, however, the Secretary of State has to exercise his discretion concerning action to remedy the harmful effects which it identifies. He receives briefing from his own officials and those of the Office of Fair Trading, both on the strength of the case made by the Commission, and on the advisability of any remedies proposed; and where other government departments have an interest in the case, he may consult the ministers concerned. His officials may consult the parties affected concerning the practicability of remedies, but except for the *1989 Beer* case, Secretaries of State have not become involved in direct negotiations with the parties. The negotiations which occurred in that case were, however, the outcome of intensive public relations and parliamentary lobbying campaigns, the success of which reflected the exceptional financial and political strength of 'the Beerage'. Since those special circumstances are unlikely to be repeated, that case cannot be regarded as having established a precedent.

G   THE CIVIL COURTS

As has been noted, the criminal courts have no jurisdiction under British competition law, although breaches of orders of the Restrictive Practices Court or of undertakings given to the Court can lead to heavy fines, or imprisonment of the firms' directors, for contempt of court. The Court of Appeal and the House of Lords have jurisdiction to hear appeals against decisions of the Restrictive Practices Court. Civil actions may also be taken against those who operate an unregistered registrable agreement, but such actions have also been rare. Under the common law doctrine of *Restraint of Trade,* the courts may declare certain restrictive agreements void, and award damages to those adversely affected by them (see Whish, 1988, Chapter 2) but few actions have been taken in recent years. No other legal remedies are at present available to those who suffer damages as a result of breaches of British competition law.

Jurisdiction under the Treaty of Rome

The courts do, however, have jurisdiction to make injunctions in respect of possible breaches of Articles 85 and 86 of the Treaty of Rome. The Commission have from time to time expressed the wish that complainants would make more use of the national courts for that purpose, and the competition authorities in most member states are empowered to do so. No such powers are available to the Office of Fair Trading and British firms have made little use of the courts for that purpose. In one or two 'spoiling actions' ostensibly designed to cause delay, firms have sought injunctions against hostile takeover bids on the grounds that they would be in breach of the Treaty (e.g. *Argyll 1987, Plessey 1988*). In each case the purpose of the injunction was ostensibly to hold up the merger until the Commission had pronounced upon it. Both cases failed on the grounds of balance of convenience, but the question of jurisdiction was not challenged. The courts also appear to be able to award damages for breaches of the Treaty, and thus to provide a remedy which is not available from the Community institutions (*Garden Cottage 1983*).

Judicial Review

The civil courts can also exercise a degree of supervision over the regulatory authorities themselves. In common with the actions of other regulatory authorities, the competition policy decisions of the Secretary of State, the Director-General of Fair Trading and the Monopolies Commission may be challenged in the High Court under a procedure which is termed *judicial review*. The permissible grounds for such a challenge are, however, strictly limited. It has been ruled that:

> proceedings for judicial review are not concerned with the correctness of the decision ... but with the means by which the decision was reached. It is no part of the court's function in such proceedings to make a new decision ... but to consider the legitimacy of the process by which the decision was reached, the relevance or validity of the considerations of which account was taken, and the admissibility or probative value of the evidence upon which the decision was based. (*ICI 1986*)

That statement followed rulings in the earlier *Tameside* and *Evans* cases that it is not the purpose of judicial review to substitute the opinion of the judiciary for that of the authority constituted by law to decide the matters in question, a point which was later confirmed by the House of Lords in the following terms

> a court is entitled to substitute its own opinion for that of a person to whom the decision has been entrusted only if the decision is so aberrant that it cannot be classed as rational. (*South Yorkshire Transport 1993*)

In the *Padfield* case, however, Lord Reid said that if the minister so uses his discretion as to thwart or run counter to the policy and objects of the relevant Act, then the law would be very defective if persons aggrieved were not entitled to the protection of the court.

An applicant for judicial review first applies for leave from the Divisional Court of the Queen's Bench Division of the High Court, supporting his application with affidavits setting out the matters on which he relies. If leave is granted, the applicant then applies for review by notice of motion and this, with the affidavits, is served on the body whose conduct is to be reviewed, and other interested parties may also be served with proceedings and given the opportunity to appear. The body whose conduct is under review then replies with its own affidavits.

The matter then goes to trial before the Divisional Court, which takes its decisions on the basis of the affidavit evidence and of submissions and arguments by Counsel. Leave may be given to appeal to the Court of Appeal and, occasionally, to the House of Lords. Even if the court finds in his favour an applicant for review is not entitled as of right to relief, but must rely upon the discretion of the Courts.

Broadly speaking, there are three grounds for review which may be described as illegality, irrationality and procedural impropriety.

Illegality has been taken to mean that 'the decision-maker must understand correctly the law that regulates his decision-making power and must give effect to it' (*Civil Service Unions 1985*). Illegality was successfully alleged in an exceptional case involving the Monopolies and Mergers Commission in which its Chairman had acted on his own in taking a decision which could legally be taken only by the Commission as a whole, or by the Group concerned (*Argyll 1986*). In that case the court exercised its discretion not to grant the complainant any relief, after taking account of effects upon other parties. In another case, illegality was unsuccessfully alleged on the grounds that the Commission should have considered a merger proposal in the form in which it was originally referred and not on the proposals as they developed in the course of the inquiry (*Air Europe 1987*).

Irrationality has been defined as:

> a decision which is so outrageous in its defiance of logic or of accepted moral standards that no sensible person who applied his mind to the question to be decided could have arrived at it. (*Civil Service Unions 1985*)

Failure to give reasons for a decision (which under Community law would render that decision void) does not under English law justify the imputation of irrationality. Over-ruling such an imputation by the Divisional Court, Lord Keith (giving judgement in the House of Lords) said that:

> It was not submitted to your Lordships that there was any general duty to give reasons for a decision in all cases ... The absence of reasons for a decision when there is no duty to give them cannot of itself provide support for the suggested irrationality of the decision. (*Lonrho* 1979)

Confirming the Civil Service Unions definition, although in somewhat less sweeping terms, Lord Keith went on to say:

The only significance of the absence of reasons is that, if all other known facts and circumstances point overwhelmingly in favour of a different decision, the decision-maker has no reason to complain if the Court draws the inference that he had no rational reasons for his decision.

The Director-General of Fair Trading and the Monopolies and Mergers Commission are required by law to give reasons for their decisions, but the above rulings appear to confirm that there is little prospect of successfully challenging their decisions on matters of substance. The Secretary of State is under no such duty and can therefore place himself in an even safer position.

The adoption of faulty methods of analysis might be interpreted either as irrationality, or as constituting an independent ground of judicial review. A claim by a brewer that the Commission had taken account of irrelevant factors and failed to take account of relevant factors in its analysis of beer prices was found by the Court to be unconvincing and was dismissed (*Matthew Brown 1987*), but that claim had not been central to the applicant's case.

Procedural irregularity is interpreted as the adoption of a procedure which breaches the laws of natural justice, and is thus unfair to the parties which are affected. In that connection also, the courts have adopted a restrictive definition:

> The question in each case is whether the Commission has adopted a procedure so unfair that no reasonable commission or group would have adopted it, so that it can be said to have acted with manifest unfairness. (*Matthew Brown 1987*)

The courts have, moreover, been prepared to countenance a degree of unfairness when it appeared to be necessary in order for the authorities to perform their duties. In the *Elders/Allied Lyons* case, the Commission had notified Elders that it considered that it would be necessary, in order to obtain Allied's comments, to supply Allied with sensitive confidential information which Elders had provided. Elders complained that their interests had not been sufficiently taken into account. Mann J. considered that if fairness alone had been in question, Elders case would be a powerful one. But the problem arose in the context of a statutory investigation, and the Commission's conclusion was that they could not perform their investigative function without obtaining Allied's comments on the information. He concluded that the Commission was:

correct in subordinating a perceived detriment to Elders to their judgement of how best to perform their statutory function. (*Elders 1987*)

In the case referred to above, it was complained that the Commission
had acted unfairly in not letting Matthew Brown have evidence which
had been provided late in the inquiry, thus – so it was claimed – depriving
them of the opportunity of submitting further evidence of their own
on that point. Macpherson J. commented that:

> It is wrong in my judgement to impose upon the Commission any
> such uniform requirement that every piece of material put before the
> Commission which may in any way influence their report must go
> to all parties or even to the opposing main participants in the bid.

From the cases reviewed it is clear that, although the British competition authorities are subject to supervision by the courts – especially
in regard to natural justice – the courts are most reluctant to take decisions which limit their discretion in performing their statutory duties.

H   ORGANISATIONAL INTERACTIONS

From the foregoing it is evident that the conduct of a British business
can fall within the jurisdiction of any of seven organisations, the Department of Trade and Industry, three other competition authorities,
and three courts of law. Moreover the rules concerning the disclosure
of confidential information about companies (summarised at Annex 1)
do not, in general, prevent the passage of such information among
those organisations. Since many cases involve two or more of those
organisations, possible interactions among them may be important.
Interactions involving the Secretary of State and the British courts have
been described in sections F and G of this chapter, and this section is
concerned with other interactions involving the Office of Fair Trading
and the Monopolies and Mergers Commission.

The Office of Fair Trading and the European Commission

As had been noted, the Office of Fair Trading acts as the United Kingdom
Competent Authority for the purpose of Regulation 17 of the EU (although
for some purposes that function falls to the Department of Trade and
Industry) and appoints a representative to the Advisory Committee on

Restrictive Practices and Monopolies. In those capacities the Office is entitled under Article 10 of Regulation 17 to receive copies of notifications and applications for negative clearance together with the most important documents lodged with the Commission for the purpose of decisions under Articles 85 and 86; and to be consulted before such decisions are made. The Commission in its turn is entitled under Article 11 to receive from the Office any information which is necessary to enable it to carry out its duties.

In principle, the Commission is also entitled under Article 13 to require the Office to undertake investigations in the United Kingdom on its behalf, although in practice this power has not been used.

There are few indications as yet that either authority has had any strong influence upon the policy followed by the other. The practical importance of liaison between the Office and the Commission probably lies mainly in efforts to avoid duplication and possible conflict in dealing with those cases in which their jurisdiction overlaps. (Parallel investigations under Community and national law are permitted under some circumstances (*Wilhelm 1969*)).

Of crucial importance to the relations between the two authorities is, however, the question of priority of jurisdiction. It has been established that a practice condemned under Community law cannot be exempted under national law, but the question whether a national authority can prohibit a practice which has been cleared by the European Commission has, at the time of writing, yet to be put to the test.

The Monopolies and Mergers Commission and the European Commission

There are no formal lines of communication between the Monopolies and Mergers Commission and the European Commission, but interaction between those bodies is nevertheless likely to assume increasing importance. The Monopolies and Mergers Commission has recognised its obligation to give effect to Community law in dealing with the rights and obligations which arise from its provisions (*Beer 1989*). In that case, it nevertheless ruled against certain practices which had been exempted by a Community Regulation. It rejected the argument that implementation of its recommendations would place the United Kingdom in breach of the Treaty of Rome, partly on the grounds that the Regulation enabled the European Commission to withdraw their exemption under circumstances such as appeared to arise in that case. But it also argued that:

under the general principles of Community law we are not prevented from considering what action, if any, should appropriately be taken to remedy identified adverse effects in the United Kingdom. However, we also recognise the duty of co-operation legally incumbent on all member states under the Treaty of Rome, which may involve consultation with the Community over proposed national measures, especially where the nature of such measures may affect the application of directly applicable Community Regulations. The European Courts have indicated in a recent case that if member states perceive or encounter unforeseen difficulties in implementing decisions of the Commission which may have been overlooked by the Commission, these may be submitted for consideration by the Commission together with proposals for suitable amendments. The duty of genuine co-operation on member states of the Community and its institutions requires them to work together in good faith to seek to overcome such difficulties whilst fully observing the Treaty provisions. There is also the question of whether a member state may legally adopt national legislation imposing more stringent restrictions in matters of competition law than are required under corresponding Community legislation. However, this is not an issue which affects the nature of our role or our recommendations. If and to the extent that issue arises in the future, it is open to the Secretary of State to consult with the Community on those of our recommendations to which Regulation 1984/83 or other Community legislation relate.

It has increasingly become the practice to consult the European Commission at an early stage in an inquiry, having consulted the main parties and considered any objections to doing so. In principle, the Monopolies and Mergers Commission is free to make recommendations which could not legally be put into effect, but in practice they may be expected to act in recognition of the legal position, once it has been established.

The Office of Fair Trading and the Monopolies and Mergers Commission

Interaction between the Office and the Commission takes place in two directions. The Office makes or recommends references to the Commission, and it is often made responsible for giving effect to those recommendations of the Commission which are accepted by the Secretary of State. However, the Director-General also advises the Secretary of State whether to accept the recommendations of the Commission. Office representatives normally give evidence to the Commission at the opening and at the conclusion of inquiries under the Competition and Fair Trading Acts, but the passage of information between them on individual cases is to some extent limited by the need to reassure businessmen concerning the handling of sensitive information. Joint seminars are used to exchange views on matters of theory and policy.

The Office does not consult the Commission before deciding whether to refer a case to them, but it does take account of any precedents which appear to have been established by previous Commission findings in order to avoid taking up time with fruitless inquiries.

Interactions with the Utilities Regulators

The regulators of each of the regulated public utilities (Electricity, Gas, Water, and Telecoms) have the power to make references to the Commission and the companies themselves may appeal to the Commission against decisions by their regulators. The Office of Fair Trading has no role in that connection, but the public utilities are not excluded from their remit. The consequent overlapping of jurisdiction between the Office and the regulators is dealt with informally on the tacit understanding that the utilities are not to suffer double jeopardy.

ANNEX 3.1

Confidentiality

Information cannot be withheld from the regulatory authorities on the grounds that its disclosure would be harmful to its provider. However, there are certain safeguards concerning its subsequent disclosure.

European Community Practice
Article 20 of Regulation 17 requires the Commission and member states not to disclose information of the kind covered by the obligation of professional secrecy. Where the Commission considers disclosure to be necessary to its investigation, it must give advance warning to the owner, who may then apply to the European Court to prevent it. Article 21 requires the Commission to publish the names of the parties and the main content of every decision, but in doing so, it is required to

'have regard to the legitimate interest of undertakings in the protection of their business secrets'. The prohibition must be presumed not to apply to the disclosure of information to the Competent Authorities of member states nor to members of the Advisory Committee on Restrictive Practices and Monopolies, both of whom are entitled to be informed under the provisions of Article 11. The use which they may make of the information is, however, limited by Article 20 which requires that the information shall be used only for the purpose of the relevant request or investigation.

The Complementary Note to Regulation 27 invites those submitting notifications and applications for negative clearance to put confidential information in a separate annex and to give reasons why it should not be published.

United Kingdom Practice
Section 133 of the Fair Trading Act 1973, Section 41 of the Restrictive Trade Practices Act 1976 and Section 19 of the Competition Act 1980 require that information obtained under those acts shall not be disclosed without the permission of the business concerned, except in pursuance of a community obligation or for the purpose of facilitating the performance of any of the functions under those Acts of the Director-General of Fair Trading, the Monopolies and Mergers Commission, the Secretary of State for Trade and Industry, or any other minister. (See for example the *Elders* case referred to in section G of Chapter 3.) The prohibition does not apply to disclosure which is made for the purposes of civil or criminal legal proceedings under the Acts. The prohibition is in any case not absolute because it expressly does not limit the content of the reports of the Director-General or the Monopolies and Mergers Commission nor the particulars which are entered upon the register of restrictive practices (but the Secretary of State can direct that commercial sensitive information be put on a part of the register which is not open to public inspection). Similar provisions apply under the privatisation acts.

It is the invariable practice of the British competition authorities to invite the providers of information to indicate any parts of it which they wish not to be disclosed. This is done during the drafting of their reports, as a part of the 'putting back' procedures. In making its reports, the Commission has a statutory duty under Section 82(1) of the Fair Trading Act 1973 and Section 16(1) of the Competition Act 1980 to have regard for the need for excluding, so far as that is practicable, matters the publication of which might in its opinion seriously and prejudicially affect the interests of those concerned. Where those sections refer to a body of persons there is, however, the proviso: 'unless in the opinion of the Commission ... the inclusion of that matter relating specifically to that body is necessary for the purposes of the report'. Using his powers under Section 83 of the Fair Trading Act and Section 17 of the Competition Act, the Secretary of State may then arrange for the excision from the published report of any passages whose publication would in his opinion be against the public interest. Representations from firms on such matters are treated sympathetically, and many of the published reports exhibit blank spaces where such excisions have been made.

Part II
Competition Policy in Practice

4 Objectives and Strategies

A INTRODUCTION

The legislation and procedures summarised in the foregoing chapters provide all that a businessman needs to know about the authorities' treatment of some business practices, such as resale price maintenance. In those cases, reference to the legislation itself, or to one of the more detailed guides which are available, may suffice. More commonly, however, it will be necessary to supplement that information with the guidance which is available from past cases. The extent to which it is necessary to go beyond what is available in the legislation and official guides to it differs, however, between the competition policy of the EU and that of the UK. The reasons for this are discussed in section E of this chapter.

In reviewing the EU's treatment of various business practices in the following four chapters, the guidance provided by official regulations, notices and reports is drawn on where available, and cases are referred to only where such guidance is lacking. Those documents are not quoted in full, but sources are given to enable readers to pursue particular aspects in more detail.

In attempting to throw light upon the treatment of business practices by the British authorities, more reliance has had to be placed upon individual cases, particularly those reported on by the Monopolies and Mergers Commission. The process of extracting references to specific practices from those reports necessarily involves taking the Commission's decisions out of context. Attention is drawn to facts which may have influenced those decisions, but intangible factors, such as the Commission's perceptions of the plausibility of the evidence before them, could not be assessed. It would, therefore, be prudent to examine the report concerned in any instance where the assessment of the treatment of a practice appears to place substantial weight upon a particular case.

B OBJECTIVES

Because of the similarities in the objectives which they serve, it has been to a large degree possible to regard the decisions of the European

Commission and those of the British authorities as complementary. Both systems are concerned with the promotion of competition and both systems provide for the balancing of that objective against other effects upon economic efficiency. But the virtually unlimited *public interest* objective enables account to be taken in the British system of considerations unrelated to competition or economic efficiency. There have in the past been numerous examples of the intrusion of non-competition into British mergers policy, as noted in section E of Chapter 6, but they can probably be regarded as transitory episodes which are unlikely to be repeated. There have also been pressures on the European Commission to take account of the need to preserve the Union's *social and economic cohesion* as required by Article 2 of the Treaty, but they have so far had no material effect.

The Interests of National Suppliers

Conflicts between the interests of British firms with those of others in the EU have seldom arisen but there have been cases in which a group conducting an inquiry has appeared to equate the public interest with the interest of a particular British supplier. Few of those cases have raised European issues, but conflicts have arisen on one or two occasions. Thus, among the 'important beneficial results' of an airline merger was the expectation that it would:

> strengthen the competitive position of BA, which is the only British company competing with major foreign airlines worldwide. (*BA/B Cal 1987*, par 8.66)

It is hardly surprising that the European Commission took a different view, and that it imposed more stringent conditions upon the merger than had been necessary to satisfy the British authorities.

A ministerial attempt in the early 1990s to establish a presumption against acquisitions by foreign state-controlled firms was rejected by the Monopolies and Mergers Commission, as noted in section F of Chapter 6.

Policy toward state aids and mergers can also give rise to conflicts with national policies. For example, the European Commission intervened in the acquisition by British Aerospace of the government-owned Rover car company, and in DAF's acquisition of the Government's stake in Leyland Trucks, and brought about substantial reductions in the Government's grants to Rover and Leyland. The European Commission have sometimes come under pressure from member states to take account of the commercial interests of nationally important companies. Their prohibition of a merger between ATR and de Havilland led to protests from the French and Italian Governments and a resolution by the European Parliament in 1991, and that issue may assume fresh importance when the mergers regulation comes under review in 1996.

Foreign Bidders

Another possible source of conflict is the attitude which has sometimes been taken by the Monopolies and Mergers Commission to the nationality of the bidder for a British company. One merger report contains the statement that:

> Foreign shareholders are less likely to attach importance to matters which may affect United Kingdom interests. (*Kuwait/BP 1988*, par 8.10)

The fact that the bidder was a member of a particularly damaging cartel was, however, the major consideration in that case. In an earlier case involving a British clearing bank, the group concerned adopted a presumption that an overseas parent would be responsive to the policy requirements of its home government rather than to those of the UK government, or to the interests and needs of the people here. That presumption was, however, considered to be rebuttable, depending on the circumstances of particular cases (*Hongkong & Shanghai Bank 1982*). That sentiment appears to have been reflected in the 15 per cent restriction initially placed by the government on foreign holdings of shares in Rolls Royce, which aroused the opposition of the European Commission.

Generally speaking, however, the British authorities have taken the view that the nationality of the bidder in a merger case is irrelevant. That view was reinforced by the Government's vigorous defence of its decision not to refer the Nestlé bid for Rowntree. On that occasion one minister dismissed the question of nationality of the bidder as 'chauvinistic nonsense' (Kenneth Clarke in the House of Commons, 8 June 1988).

A merger between a British and an overseas firm can fall within the jurisdiction of the European Commission if it is likely to affect trade between member states, even if the overseas partner comes from outside the Community (as in the case of the Minorco bid for Consolidated

Gold Fields). The Commission's treatment of such a case is likely to be determined by its effect upon competition, without regard for the nationality of the bidder.

Overseas Markets

Restrictive trade practices which are operated by British firms in overseas markets fall within the jurisdiction of the European Commission under Article 85 of the Treaty of Rome if they are likely to affect trade between member states. Such practices fall outside the jurisdiction of the Restrictive Practices Court. Under the existing Restrictive Trade Practices Act, however, a purely domestic restriction can be defended on the grounds that its removal would cause a reduction in exports. That defence has succeeded in only one case (*Water-Tube Boilers 1959*), and the Court has subsequently rejected similar arguments.

Restrictive practices operated abroad by British firms can, however, be referred to the Monopolies and Mergers Commission if there is considered to be a *monopoly situation in exports* (as defined in Section 8 of the Fair Trading Act – see section C of Chapter 2). In the last three cases involving market sharing or price-fixing in export markets, however, those practices were found not to be against the public interest (*Ceramic Sanitaryware 1978; Electricity Supply Meters 1979; Insulated Wires and Cables 1979*). Monopoly references since 1979 have been restricted to the supply of goods or services in the United Kingdom.

One restrictive agreement between British and foreign companies has come to the attention of both authorities. The *Voluntary Restraint Agreement* between the Society of Motor Manufacturers and Traders and the Japanese Automobile Manufacturers Association has been held responsible for the high prices of cars in Britain (*Cars 1992*) and attempts by the European Commission to evade that issue have been condemned by the Court (*VRAs 1994*).

C　STRATEGY: STRUCTURE AND BEHAVIOUR

It has been noted that in the design of any system of competition policy, a balance has to be struck between the strategy of limiting monopoly power by regulating market structure, and the strategy of avoiding economic damage by discouraging anticompetitive behaviour. Differences in that respect between the UK and EU may give rise to conflicts. Under British law, for example, the acquisition of even a very substantial measure of market power can be approved if there is no evidence of a prospect of abuse. Under European law, on the other hand, a defence based upon the absence of such evidence has been specifically rejected (*Continental Can 1973*).

Persuasive arguments can be advanced in favour of either strategy. These are considered briefly below.

Mergers Policy

It can be argued on the one hand that, in the absence of an effective mergers policy, regulation of anti-competitive behaviour gives firms a motive to seek market power by acquisitions. It is a paradox of competition policy that practices such as price-fixing, which are unlawful if they are the subject of an agreement between two firms, become acceptable if those same firms come under common ownership or control. If firms are not to be encouraged to escape the regulation of such practices by joining together, consistency of policy would thus apparently require a control over mergers which is no less strict than that applied to concerted practices. Such arguments have frequently been advanced by the European Commission as grounds for extending their powers to regulate mergers which have a 'community dimension'.

On the other hand, it can be argued that the threat of takeover is a spur to managerial efficiency, and that the acquisition of even a very substantial degree of market power by a merger is not necessarily a cause for concern, because it cannot be assumed that such market power will be abused, and because remedies are available for any abuse of market power that does occur. Since abuse can be avoided, there is thus a case for giving more weight to the promise that a merger may increase productive efficiency than to the danger of abuse. The influence of such arguments can be detected in some of the reports of the Monopolies and Mergers Commission.

Broader Implications

Carried to its logical conclusion, the latter line of argument has implications going beyond the control of mergers. Its acceptance would point to a permissive policy towards all practices which could result in an increase in productive efficiency, with the sole exception of those practices which actually harm the ultimate consumer. Given a guarantee that the abuse of market power could be prevented by regulation, it could further be argued that a reduction in competition is not in itself a cause for concern. Attempts to prevent the acquisition of market power by mergers or by the formation of cartels could therefore be abandoned, and regulatory intervention could be confined to those measures which are necessary to prevent the exploitation of the consumer. Such, in effect, is the policy which has been proposed in the United States by some members of the Chicago School (see the passages in Bork 1978 pp. 125 and 406 which have been referred to in section D of Chapter 1). Although not taking such an extreme position, reports of the Monopolies and Mergers Commission have on several occasions cited the discretionary powers available under the Competition Act in justification of a presumption that market power would not be abused.

D   STRATEGY: POLICY DEVELOPMENT AND COMMUNICATION

Although there are unlikely to be radical differences between the treatment of business practices by the EU and the British authorities, the sources of information which are drawn upon in the following four chapters are affected by the radically different strategies which they have adopted towards the evolution of policy and towards the problem of communicating policy messages to businessmen.

The European Union Approach

The approach adopted by the EU has been stated in the following terms.

> The Commission's administrative practice, supported by the Court of Justice in its judgments, has made it possible gradually to introduce a body of rules governing fair conduct which give market operators an idea of how they must behave if equality of opportunity, freedom of access to business and freedom of choice are to be guaranteed within the common market. (Comp Rep 8, 1979)

The European Court of Justice has had an important effect upon the development of policy. As noted in section B of Chapter 3, it may over-rule a decision of the Commission or a regulation adopted by the Council on the grounds that it is inadequately reasoned. That power of review has affected the conduct of the Commission's business in two ways. Firstly, it has prompted it to take and justify its decisions with a view to having to defend them before the Court. Secondly, it has enabled it to treat successfully defended decisions as contributions to the substantive law of the EU. Where possible, it has sought to embody the effects of such decisions into regulations – a process which has involved it in sometimes lengthy negotiations in the Advisory Committee and in the Council.

The adoption of a strategy of progressive codification has to some extent been a matter of necessity, since the Commission would have little hope of reducing its backlog purely on a case-by-case basis. The selection of practices for investigation and subsequent codification has thus been influenced by the need to reduce that backlog by granting block exemptions. A drawback of that strategy has been a tendency to give priority to practices according to their volume rather than their importance. On the other hand, it has had the advantage from a businessman's standpoint of providing a motive for consistency and predictability of treatment. Codification also reduces the need for a businessman to consult and analyse case law in order to find whether, and under what circumstances, a particular practice is likely to be considered permissible.

EU competition policy has thus evolved gradually through critical review, open debate and the embodiment of accumulated experience into explicit rules and guidelines. That process of evolution is now set to continue.

The United Kingdom Approach

Open debate and the establishment of explicit rules and guidelines play a comparatively small part in British competition policy. Review by the courts is rare, and is nowadays confined to procedural issues. The former role of the Restrictive Practices Court has given way to administrative procedures which are not open to inspection or review.

The reports of the Monopolies and Mergers Commission do occasionally contain general statements of policy, but the commission normally conducts its business on a case-by-case basis, and a report is typically confined to a detailed examination and evaluation of the circumstances of the referred case. The Commission does not consider itself to be bound by precedent, and cross-references to previous cases are rare. An investigating group usually concentrates upon the merits of the case under consideration, without making any attempt to convey any general message to businessmen other than those directly concerned in that case.

E TRANSPARENCY

European Union Policy

In addition to the competition policy articles in the Treaty, and the reporting of decisions in the Official Journal, extensive material is published by the Commission, as noted in Annex 4.1 below. Many of the legally-binding regulations which are issued are in effect codifications of previous case law, and these are supplemented by non-binding Commission Notices intended to interpret the regulations and to relate and explain the Commission's decisions. In addition, the Commission have responded to complaints about the lack of transparency of its informal negotiations with firms by publishing, where possible, draft undertakings offered in the course of those negotiations for comment by interested parties.

Reports of decisions in the Official Journal (L series) tend to be confined to matters directly relevant to those decisions, and have been criticised for not giving sufficient background material.

United Kingdom Policy

The fact that the Monopolies and Mergers Commission is not bound by precedent, limits the extent to which its decisions can be explained in official publications other than the reports of individual cases. The British material referred to in Annex 4.1 below does not, therefore, offer much guidance concerning the likely treatment of particular practices, but consists mainly of factual summaries of legislation and cases, and descriptions of organisations and procedures. No attempt is made in the publicly available material to explain the rationale connecting related recommendations but the precedents handbook presents factual summaries for use by members of the Commission. The recently introduced register of undertakings is likely, in the future, to throw light upon the hitherto opaque conduct of the negotiations between firms and the Office of Fair Trading.

Reports of inquiries present very extensive background material, usually following a format unrelated to the issues arising in any particular case, together with a separately drafted statement of the Commission's conclusions.

ANNEX 4.1 OFFICIAL PUBLICATIONS

European Union

The Official Journal, L series (legislation, daily) Regulations, decisions and directives reproduced in full on all topics, a competition decision typically covers 10 to 80 pages.

The Official Journal, C series (communications, daily) Information, Commission notices, bald statements of Court judgements and Commission decisions.

Bulletin of the European Communities (monthly about 100 pages). Short (10 to 30 line) summaries of Commission decisions &c on competition and all other topics.

Report on Competition Policy (annual, 330 to 500 pages). Summaries of all Commission and Court decisions, detailed analyses of the treatment of selected aspects of mergers and business practices, summaries of competition policy activities in member states.

Bulletin Supplements, e.g. Community merger control law (57 pages) Regulations, Commission notices, explanatory notes.

EEC Competition Policy in the Single Market (70 pages) A summary of law and procedures.

Competition Policy Newsletter (quarterly, about 80 pages) More detailed summaries and commentaries.

Competition Law in the European Communities. Volume 1A. Rules applicable to undertakings; the situation at 30 June 1994. A detailed survey of the legislation.

Merger Control Law in the European Union 1995, A survey of legislation and leading cases.

European Community Competition Policy 1994 (47 pages) Policy analysis and discussion.

Also obtainable, subject to commercial confidentiality: Copies of undertakings and selected comfort letters.

The Office of Fair Trading

Report of the Director-General (annual, 70 to 90 pages). A personal statement followed by factual summaries of UK competition policy cases and important EU cases (together with material relating to consumer protection).

An Outline of United Kingdom Competition Policy (20 pages).

Guides

1. *Monopolies and Anti-Competitive Practices.*
2. *Register of Undertakings and Orders*
3. *Restrictive Agreements*
4. *Restrictive Trade Practices*
5. *Restrictive Practices in the Bus Industry*
6. *Cartels: Detection and Remedies – A Guide for Purchasers*
7. *Cartels: Detection and Remedies – A Guide for Local Authorities*
8. *Mergers*
9. *Guide for Rail Mergers*
10. *Mergers: The Contents of Submissions*

The Monopolies and Mergers Commission

Reports of inquiries: (Typically 70 to 500 pages). Summary, detailed factual chapters, separately drafted conclusions.

Annual Review (30–40 pages). Chairman's statement, list of members and senior staff, summaries of reports.

The Role of the Commission (28 pages). Brief factual summaries of legislation and procedures.

Fact Sheets (4–5 pages). Brief factual statements:

1. *The Monopolies and Mergers Commission*
2. *The Commission and its Members*
3. *Recent Commission Reports*
4. *Merger References*
5. *Monopoly References*
6. *References Other Than Merger and Monopoly References*

Guidance Handbook (unpublished). Mainly definitional, covering market definition, profitability, marginal costs, etc. Supplement *Assessing Competition* (12 pages, published).

Precedents Handbook (unpublished). Exhaustive summaries of past Commission treatments of each of a range of issues and practices.

The Department of Trade and Industry

Competition Policy: How it Works (18 pages). Describes procedures and gives policy contacts.

Press releases. Give ministerial references and responses to MMC reports.

5 The Treatment of Market Power

A INTRODUCTION

The Importance of Market Power

Market power gives its possessor a degree of choice concerning the prices he may charge and the consequent levels of sales which he may expect. It is the crucial concept of competition theory because it is a measure of the economic loss which can be imposed upon the rest of the community by distorting consumer choice away from the cost-related basis which rules under pure competition. It is also of considerable importance in the practical application of many aspects of competition policy. Measures of market power, or 'dominance' often determine who comes within the scope of regulatory action. Regulatory intervention under Article 86 of the Treaty of Rome, for example, can be applied only to those who occupy a 'dominant position'; which has been defined as:

> a position of economic strength enjoyed by an undertaking which enables it to hinder the maintenance of effective competition in the relevant market by allowing it to behave to an appreciable extent independently of its competitors and customers. (*Michelin v Commission 1983*)

Although the Court has not indicated how the phrase 'to an appreciable extent' is to be interpreted, there is a clear implication that the jurisdiction of the Commission depends upon its ability to establish that the undertaking possesses a sufficient degree of market power.

The methods used to measure market power are thus important in determining who is to come within the scope of regulation. They may also have a strong influence upon the treatment of those who do. There is no presumption in UK or EU competition policy that market power is harmful in itself, but measures of market power are widely used as indicators of the magnitude of possible losses of allocative efficiency. They can be of decisive importance in cases in which such losses have to be weighed against possible gains in productive efficiency.

97

The Measurement of Market Power

The measurement of market power raises considerable difficulties, however. Market power is not solely a characteristic of its possessor, but depends also upon the reactions of his customers. Customers may react in a variety of ways. If they respond to an increase in the price of one product by switching their purchases to a close substitute, their behaviour thereby limits both the exercise of market power to increase the price of that product, and the amount of economic damage that it can do. If, on the other hand, they respond by switching some of their purchases to an entirely different category of product, resources are misallocated to a greater extent and there may be a substantial loss of economic welfare. A price increase which leads to the substitution of one type of thermal insulation for another is clearly of less significance than one which leads to a switch of expenditure into energy consumption. If, however, customers are relatively insensitive to price changes, a price increase may result mainly in a transfer of resources to the producer, with a minimal distortion of expenditure patterns and little loss of total welfare. An increase in bread prices, for example, may have little effect on bread consumption.

A supplier's market power may also be reduced or eliminated if his customers enjoy market power as buyers. It has been noted that the very high degree of concentration in food manufacturing which has developed in Britain has not conferred excessive market power upon the big suppliers because of the countervailing buying power of the large supermarket chains (*Discounts to Retailers 1981*). The elimination by mergers of all competition in the United Kingdom safety glass industry was found not to be against the public interest because of the bargaining power of that industry's main customers (*Flat Glass 1968*, par 293). Similarly, a merger of suppliers of personalised cheques which would give the combined firm a 40 per cent market share was found not to be against the public interest because of the buying power of the banks, who were their only customers (*Norton Opax/McCorquodale 1986*).

The extent of a supplier's market power depends also upon the reactions of his rivals. If the originator of a price increase is looked upon as a price leader, other suppliers may match his increase. Otherwise he will lose sales to them to the extent that their products are seen as substitutes for his. He may also face the danger that his price increase may prompt the entry of new producers into the market.

Market Shares

A measure which can act as partial surrogate for market power is obtained by calculating a supplier's share of the relevant product market. The usefulness of that measure depends, however, upon the procedure used to establish the definition of the relevant market. Too narrow a definition would exclude substitutes which limit market power so that the possession of a particular share would thus tend to give a misleadingly high impression of market power. (The true market power represented by a 100 per cent share in the market for bananas, for example, would be limited by the willingness of customers to accept other forms of fresh fruit as substitutes.) Too broad a definition would include products which have little influence upon the market for the product in question, and would thus lead to a misleadingly low market share.

The United States Department of Justice's 1992 merger guidelines define an *anti-trust market* in the following terms:

> a product or group of products and a geographical area in which it is sold, such that a hypothetical, profit-maximising firm, not subject to price regulation, that was the only present and future seller of those products in that area would impose a small but significant and non-transitory increase in price above prevailing or likely future levels.

Because the 'small but significant' increase has normally been taken as 5 per cent, that criterion has come to be known as the *five per cent test*. The implication is that if the hypothetical monopolist is unable to raise prices even by that amount, there must be strong competitive forces, such as the availability of substitutes, which prevent him from doing so. In practice, of course, it will usually be possible to envisage a succession of product categories, some of the broader of which offer an implausible market definition because of the weakness of the implied restraining force. (Our hypothetical banana monopolist might have less than a 1 per cent share of the market for all food, but that percentage would greatly understate his market power.) The five per cent test is a recognition that there is no unique solution to the problem of market definition, and that an arbitrary cut-off is therefore necessary. Here, as elsewhere in competition policy, the criterion for effectiveness is consistency rather than correctness.

The market share under the five per cent test depends upon buyer's sensitivity to the price of the product or, in the jargon, upon its *own-*

price elasticity. That quantity is, however, largely determined by the extent to which a price increase would prompt buyers to switch to a substitute, or its *cross-price elasticity* with that substitute. When attempting to make a broad qualitative judgement it is often easier to think directly in terms of likely switching.

The five per cent test is used also to determine the geographical extent of the market which should be used for market share assessments. The determining factor is the extent to which buyers would respond to a price increase by switching to other locations – a concept which has an obvious connection with cross-price elasticity.

The British and European competition authorities employ criteria which are less precisely defined than the five per cent test, and which differ slightly in other respects. Competitive forces other than availability of substitutes, such as buying power and entry prospects, could provide the restraints required to meet the five per cent test; but those are treated as additional factors affecting market power rather than determinants of the market used in estimating market shares. While the five per cent test is concerned exclusively with what is termed *demand-side substitution*, the estimation of market shares also takes account, where appropriate, of *supply-side substitution*. To take a rather contrived example, the market for shoes would be taken to cover the full range of shoe sizes, even though different sizes are not substitutes from a buyer's standpoint. The ability of other food manufacturers to adapt their equipment to the production of pet foods was, however, treated as facilitating entry rather than broadening the market (*Cat and Dog Foods 1977*).

B   THE MEASUREMENT OF MARKET SHARES

Market Share Criteria

EU law does not stipulate a market share criterion for dominance, but the Commission has stated that:

A dominant position can generally be said to exist once a market share to the order of 40 per cent to 45 per cent has been reached. Although this share does not in itself automatically give control of the market, if there are large gaps between the position of the firm concerned and those of its closest competitors and also other factors likely to place it at an advantage as regards competition, a dominant position may well exist ... A dominant position cannot even be ruled out in respect of market shares between 20 per cent and 40 per cent. (Comp Report 10, 1980, point 150)

There is a presumption that a merger which does not lead to a combined market share of over 25 per cent will be regarded as 'compatible with the common market' (Recital 15 of the preamble to Regulation 4064/89).

Under British law, the possession of a market share of at least 25 per cent is necessary to justify a monopoly reference – but a reference may be made if a group of firms constituting a 'complex monopoly' (as defined in Section C of Chapter 2) together hold such a share. A combined market share of 25 per cent is sufficient to justify a merger reference, although in most merger references formal use is made instead of the size of assets criterion (see section F of Chapter 2) for reasons of administrative convenience. The Commission must establish whether the criteria for its jurisdiction are met, and need not adopt the market definition contained in the reference (*Stagecoach/Lancaster City 1993*).

The Treatment of Substitutes

In principle, the process of assessing the account to be taken of substitutes involves first estimating how far their existence reduces market power, and then deciding whether that degree of reduction is to be deemed significant. In the absence of published guidelines, the only indications which are available concerning the methodology and criteria which the authorities actually adopt are those which emerge from reported cases. The outcome is reflected in various cases, either as a decision whether to include the substitute product when calculating market shares, or as a conclusion as to whether the existence of the substitute limits the danger of abuse.

In some relevant EU cases, it has been held that:

the market for bananas is distinct from that for other fresh fruit because of their distinctive qualities and because their cross-elasticity of demand with other fresh fruit is low (*United Brands 1978*);

the market for tyres for heavy commercial vehicles is distinct from that for cars and light vans because of differences in the structure of demand, but that no such distinction can be drawn between the markets for truck tyres and bus tyres (*Michelin 1983*);

the market for replacement parts is distinct from that for the same parts as originally supplied with cars or cash registers because competitive conditions are different (*Michelin 1983, Hugin 1979, Varta/Bosch 1991*);

and the market for spares for one type of cash register is distinct from those for spares for other cash registers (*Hugin 1979*);

vitamins supplied for medicinal use compete in a different market from those for the same vitamins supplied for industrial use (*Hoffman-La Roche 1979*);

the market for nylon fibres for carpet manufacture is distinct from that for other fibres because nylon is harder-wearing and substantially more costly and there is little supply-side substitutability (*Du Pont/ICI 1992*);

the market for bottled source waters is distinct from that for soft drinks because consumption patterns are substantially different (*Nestlé/Perrier 1992*);

the market for coated paper must be distinguished from that for uncoated paper although there is relatively easy supply-side substitutability, because dominance could be affected by the lack of demand-side substitutability (*Torras/Sarrio 1992*);

motorway restaurants constitute a different market from other types of restaurant because, on the demand side, they are restricted to motorway travellers and because of distinct supply-side conditions (*Accor/Wagons Lits 1992* conflicting with the UK case *Happy Eater/Little Chef* 1987 below);

there are three distinct markets for commuter aircraft with differing seat capacities, as established by economic analysis of demand patterns (*Aerospatiale/Alena/de Havilland 1991*);

the market for packaging machines for cartons was distinct from that for packaging machines for glass and plastics, because customer surveys had shown there to be a low cross-elasticity of demand between them (*Tetra Pak/Alpha Laval 1991*);

but there are not separate markets for different types of bricks, despite limited demand-side substitutability, because the costs to suppliers of switching production are insignificant (*Tarmac/Steetley 1992* apparently conflicting directly with the UK case *London Brick/Ibstock Johnson 1983* below).

The market definitions in the above cases appear to have been derived from considerations of cross-elasticity of demand, based either upon econometric evidence, or upon the reasoning that cross-elasticity must be low because few purchasers buy in both markets. The grounds adduced for resisting attempts to broaden the market definition appear to be convincing. It has to be recognised, however, that the burden of proof in those cases was effectively borne by the Commission, and that had they failed, the cases would probably have been deemed to fall outside the scope of Article 86.

In some relevant Monopolies and Mergers Commission cases it has been held that:

the market for plain biscuits is not distinct from that for sweet biscuits because the two products are handled together for the purpose of discounts, promotions and advertising; so that the creation of a 60 per cent market share for plain biscuits was not a matter for concern in view of the lower (24 per cent) share of the combined market (*Nabisco/Huntley & Palmer 1982*);

the market for fletton facing bricks supplied for use in cheap houses is distinct from the market for non-fletton bricks supplied for expensive houses; so that a merger which raised the share of the combined market for fletton and non-fletton bricks from 39 per cent to 51 per cent was not of concern because it had little effect upon shares in either of the separate markets (*London Brick/Ibstock Johnson 1983*);

the market for cabinet towels was considered in 1983 to be distinct from that for paper towels and air dryers (*Sunlight/Initial/Johnson 1983*); but in 1985 it was considered that the possibility of abuse of a 63 per cent share of the cabinet towel market would be limited by competition from paper towels and air dryers (*BET/Initial 1985*);

abuse of a market share of 92 per cent brought about by the merger of the 'Happy Eater' and 'Little Chef' chains of roadside restaurants would be prevented by competition from snack bars, pubs and filling stations (*Happy Eater/Little Chef 1987*);

the ability of suppliers of pet foods to raise prices is limited by the availability of household scraps (*Cat and Dog Foods 1977*);

there was little competition between tampons and external sanitary towels in 1980; but by 1986 competition from improved external towels and retailers' own brands – together with entry prospects – were expected to prevent abuse (*Tampons 1980 and 1986*);

the buying of trailers is a close substitute for leasing (*Tiphook/Trailerent 1990*);

pneumatic power tools are close substitutes for electric power tools (*Atlas Copco/Desoutter 1990*);

the markets for travellers cheques is distinct from that served by credit and debit cards (*Thomas Cook/ISL 1995*).

Although supply-side substitutability is not explicitly mentioned in Commission reports, products among which there is little demand-side substitutability have sometimes been grouped together in calculating market shares (e.g. *Opium Derivatives 1989* and brass extrusions in *Trellebourg/McKechnie 1990*).

In none of the reports of the above cases was there any reference to estimates of cross-elasticities. In the roadside restaurants case, responses to a questionnaire on motorists' eating habits indicated that price ranked lower in importance than cleanliness and quality, but motorists were not asked about the circumstances under which they would change their eating habits. In the bricks case, expert evidence concerning interactions between the markets for fletton and non-fletton bricks was reported, but the evidence was conflicting. No evidence concerning customer behaviour was reported in any of the other cases. It would appear from the evidence presented in those reports that most of the judgements reported were based upon introspection rather than analysis, and that different groups of commissioners may have adopted different criteria.

Geographical Coverage

The appropriate geographical area to be used in calculating market shares may depend solely upon buyer behaviour, but supply-side costs may also be relevant. In local retail distribution it will usually depend upon how far afield customers are prepared to travel in search of value for money. The wholesale market area which should be used for some products may, however, be determined by local or national differences in tastes and for others it may be influenced by supply-side considerations such as transport costs.

National markets, rather than Community-wide markets, have been considered relevant in a number of cases decided by the European Commission. Reasons included customers' reluctance to travel too far to buy food products (*Promodes/BRMC 1992*); differing consumer preferences for bottled water (*Nestle/Perrier 1992*) and for ice cream (*Unilever/Ortiz 1994*); and the high transport costs for bricks in relation to their selling price (*Tarmac/Steetley 1992*). The market for the chemicals persalts, on the other hand, was considered to be the Community because of the centralised purchasing employed by large customers, and not the world in view of a low level of imports in face of a 7 per cent external tariff (*Solvay/Laporte 1992*). Remaining trade barriers for gas pipes were considered temporarily to restrict the relevant market to Germany (*Mannesman/Hoesch 1992*) but import duties which were due to expire in the following year were not taken to restrict an otherwise community-wide market for rubber car parts (*BTR/Pirelli 1992*). There was considered to be a world market for commuter aircraft in view of buyers' purchasing policies (*Aerospatiale/Alenia/de Havilland 1991*).

Monopoly inquiries under British law are normally concerned with the UK market as a whole unless a smaller market is specified in the reference. In *Ready Mixed Concrete 1981* the Commission noted that that industry consists, not of one national market, but of a large number of local markets, but that their terms of reference did not extend to an investigation of those local markets. In *Caravan Sites 1983*, on the other hand, some consideration was given to the lack of consumer choice in the Ards peninsular, despite the fact that the reference was concerned with supply of sites in Northern Ireland as a whole.

Local market shares have assumed importance in a number of UK mergers involving the supply of services. The 25 per cent combined market share criterion for a merger reference can be applied to supply in the UK or in a 'substantial part' of it; although, as has been noted, the alternative 'size of assets' criterion is more often employed. The term 'A substantial part' has been interpreted by the House of Lords only to mean an area 'of such dimension as to make it worthy of consideration for the purposes of the Act' (*South Yorkshire Transport 1993*). The criterion used for the reference of *CWS/House of Fraser 1987* was the combined share of funeral services in Scotland as a whole, but the issue identified by the Commission was the acquisition of market shares ranging from 77 per cent to 100 per cent in Aberdeen, Falkirk and Perth. Adverse effects of a merger of pharmaceutical wholesalers were attributed to a reduction in competition in the Grampian and Highland region of Scotland (*AAH/Medicopharma 1992*) and effects on small local markets were considered relevant to a merger involving roadside posters (*Havas/Brunton Curtis 1991*). Effects upon the linen rental market in London were the reason for prohibiting another merger (*Sunlight/Initial/Johnson 1983*).

In mergers affecting retail outlets, even smaller local markets have sometimes been considered. In a merger case affecting 'tied' public houses, the Commission commented that

from the point of view of ... the effect on the consumer of increased concentration, it is not meaningful to consider an area the
size of North and West Cumbria or even one the size of a licensing
district within it. The relevant area for consumers is typically the
individual town or even village. (*Scottish & Newcastle/Matthew Brown
1985*)

In their subsequent inquiry, Petty Sessional Divisions (of which there
are approximately 600 in Great Britain) were used for the calculation
of the shares of retail outlets owned by the major brewers (*Beer 1989*).

In the case of supermarkets, however, the market shares considered
have been calculated on the basis of areas much larger than could con-
ceivably be justified on the grounds of consumer choice. Very few of the
numerous mergers involving supermarket chains have been referred to
the Commission. In those which have, market shares have been calculated on the basis of areas no smaller than the television regions (*Linfood/
Fitch Lovell 1983, Dee/Booker McConnell 1985*). In respect of cash-
and-carry depots, survey evidence showed that 80 per cent of purchases were made by customers who had travelled less than ten miles,
but the fact that a merger would increase the number of such areas in
which there would be little or no competition from 52 to 76 was not
considered to justify its prohibition (*Dee/Booker McConnell 1985*).

There have been a few UK merger cases in which a market wider
than the UK has been considered relevant. World markets were considered in *Merck/Alginates 1979* and in *Minorco/ConsGold 1989*, and
sugar imports were important in *Berisford/British Sugar 1981* and *Tate
& Lyle/Ferruzzi/Berisford 1987*. In a statement of mergers policy to a
Stock Exchange conference on 27 October 1988, the Secretary of State
for Trade and Industry said:

Some markets are confined to a part of the UK, for example the
recent Badgerline case concerning bus services in Bristol and Avon.
Bus services are a market where competition is highly localised.
Other products and services have a national, UK-wide market, for
example package holidays where competition in the market for foreign
inclusive holidays by air is mainly between UK companies. Thompson
and Horizon have a large share of this market, and there appeared
to be no mitigating factors such as competition from overseas operators. So the bid raised issues of competition and was referred.
For some products, competition comes from Europe. In a few weeks
British Steel is coming to the market as a single entity. It still has

over 60 per cent of the domestic market for finished steel products, but in the UK it is still faced by competition from other European producers. The Minorco bid for Consolidated Gold Fields was referred on competition grounds. The Director-General of Fair Trading in the usual way assessed the implication for the world-wide supply and prices of certain minerals and metals. I accepted his advice.

In illustration of the practice in the Office of Fair Trading of taking account of overseas competition, the Director-General referred to a merger between two British manufacturers of automotive bearings which gave them a combined share of 94 per cent of the UK market but which was not referred because:

> although actual import penetration was low, British car manufacturers, we thought, can without difficulty or inconvenience source their products from other countries in the EC whenever they wish. (statement reported in the *Guardian*, 12 May 1988)

In a number of other cases which were referred to the Monopolies and Mergers Commission, the existence of international competition was treated as evidence of entry prospects rather than as affecting market shares, but that choice probably arose for mainly procedural reasons.

C THE TREATMENT OF ENTRY PROSPECTS

The Influence of Entry Prospects

As has been noted, entry prospects can be crucial because they can limit the prospects of abuse to the point at which, despite the existence of high market shares, intervention by the regulatory authorities becomes unnecessary.

The existence of good entry prospects has been decisive in some monopoly cases. In a case in which a renderer of animal waste had a 44 per cent market share and was getting returns on capital employed of up to 45 per cent, it was considered difficult to attribute those profits to its monopoly position in view of the opportunities open to slaughterers to enter the rendering market. It was concluded that if the exploitation of the slaughterers by the dominant renderer was not sufficiently important to prompt such entry, it could have little effect on the public interest (*Animal Waste 1985*).

Ease of entry by other large firms into the market for instant coffee was the main reason for finding Nestlé's high profit rates not to be against the public interest (*Soluble Coffee 1991*, also discussed at 7B below). Account has also been taken of the future consequences of recent entry (*Plasterboard 1990*).

More commonly, however, *entry barriers* have figured in monopoly enquiries as contributing to market power. The European Commission have several times treated the possession of a technological lead as creating an entry barrier (*United Brands 1978, Hoffman-la Roche 1979, Michelin 1983*), (but see also the treatment of intellectual property rights at 5F below). In the UK the magnitude of the investment required for large-scale salt manufacture was among the considerations which prompted the Monopolies and Mergers Commission to recommend price control (*White Salt 1986*). Remedies designed to facilitate entry have included the agreed withdrawal of a firm from some of the more concentrated of its markets (e.g. *Air France/Sabena 1992*), and the recommended removal of import quotas (*Cars 1992*). In one case, the risk of deterring new entry was a reason for not acting against uncompetitive pricing (*Tampons 1986*).

Entry prospects have had an even more important influence in many merger cases. The costs and delays inherent in the development of a new aeroplane were among the reasons for the European Commission's first prohibition under the 1989 merger regulation (*Aerospatiale/Alenia/ de Havilland 1991*) and the obstacles to new entry into the German pay-television market were a decisive factor in *Bertelsmann/Kirch/Deutsche Telekom 1994*. The possibility of competitively-priced imports was, on the other hand, considered to justify permitting a merger between the two of the Community's largest yarn producers (*Courtaulds/SNIA 1991*) The difficulty of entry into mail-order retailing was one of the reasons for prohibiting a merger which would add to the market share of the dominant firm (*GUS/Empire 1983*). Ease of entry into cash-and-carry retailing was, on the other hand, a reason for permitting a merger which would give the merged company a 37 per cent share of all general grocery depots (*Dee/Booker McConnell 1985*). Ease of entry was also a reason for permitting the takeover by Britain's largest tour operator of its third largest tour operator, giving a combined market share of 38 per cent (*Thomson/Horizon 1989*). Obstacles to entry into the biscuit market were a factor in concluding that a proposed merger between two lesser suppliers would provide for more effective competition with the dominant United Biscuits (*Nabisco/Huntley and Palmer 1982*).

The importance of entry prospects to mergers practice was illustrated by the fact that in only one out of 22 merger cases examined by the Monopolies and Mergers Commission between 1980 and 1986, was there an adverse public interest finding in the absence of entry barriers (Littlechild, 1986).

The Assessment of Entry Prospects

A potential entrant to a market in which the dominant firm has set prices at above the competitive level must be assumed to take account of the prospect that his entry will lead to a reduction in those prices. Accordingly, he must choose between two strategies:

(a) to make a temporary incursion into the market in order to take advantage of the period during which prices remain high, and to withdraw before they fall to a level at which it is no longer profitable for him to compete; or

(b) to plan for a sustained entry, and to seek a position in which he can at least match the unit costs and quality of the dominant firm, and can thus continue to compete even after prices have been driven down to their competitive level.

(Termed, respectively, *uncommitted entry* and *committed entry*). If there is a plausible threat of either strategy being adopted, it may be assumed to deter the dominant firm from overcharging. But an established firm may be assumed to enjoy some advantages over a newcomer, and unless the dominant firm is evidently inefficient, the potential entrant may face considerable risks. Those risks can, however, be eliminated if the initial investment which is required for entry can later be recovered without loss. The market is then termed *contestable* as noted in section B of Chapter 1 and uncommitted entry is a commercially attractive strategy. Perfect contestability is rarely approached, however, and a threat of uncommitted entry is unlikely to be a plausible influence on market power. Nevertheless, the risks incurred in what is intended to be committed entry are the smaller, the lower are the net costs of entry and of exit.

The threat of entry is thus more plausible when the capital equipment required can readily be diverted from – and returned to – other markets. The high market share of a supplier of cans for preserving food was for that reason not considered to confer dominance since manufacturers of other types of can could readily adapt their equipment in order to compete in its markets (*Continental Can 1973*). Similarly, the high market shares of two pet-food suppliers were considered not to be a cause for concern, partly because the equipment used by other food manufacturers could be adapted to the production of pet foods (*Cat and Dog Foods 1977*).

If the equipment required to enable a new entrant to establish himself in the market cannot be put to other uses, the size of the investment involved may be relevant to the prospects of entry. The need for a very large initial investment need not, of course, be a barrier to entry if the market conditions offer good prospects for its recovery. On the other hand, the need for a relatively small investment can constitute a barrier where recovery prospects are poor. An entry cost of between £360 000 and £1 million was in one case considered to make entry unlikely into a market with annual sales of about £12 million a year (*MiTek/Gang-Nail 1988*).

The speed with which a new entrant can make a competitive impact is an explicit factor under the merger guidelines issued by the US Department of Justice, and a time lag of over two years is one of its entry criteria. Such *entry lags* have at several times been given explicit consideration in the decisions of the European Commission. For entry into the market for commercial aircraft the entry lag was put at six to seven years (*Aerospatiale/Alenia/de Havilland 1991*) whereas that for car parts was put at two years (*Lucas/Eaton 1991*).

The effects upon entry prospects of regulatory barriers have been recognised in a number of cases (e.g. *Accor/Wagons Lits 1992* and *Alcatel/ Telettra 1991*) and the existence of overcapacity has been taken to indicate that entry would be impracticable (e.g. *Du Pont/ICI 1992*). The authorities' treatments of the entry consequences of scale economies, brand loyalty and advertising, and intellectual property rights are each discussed in the following sections.

D   ECONOMIES OF SCALE AND OF LEARNING

The prospects that a new entrant to a market can recover his initial investment are reduced if an existing supplier enjoys scale economies which cannot be matched unless the entrant captures a very large share of that market. In the limiting case in which the costs of supplying the entire market are substantially lower when there is one supplier than when there are two, the market is said to be *a natural monopoly*. Apart from a few well-known special cases such as telephone, railway and electricity distribution networks, natural monopolies are rare. In manufacturing industry it is common for economies to continue only up to a limiting scale of production – known as the *minimum efficient size* – beyond which there is no appreciable further advantage in an increase in output. There are very few products for which the minimum efficient plant size is comparable with a market of the size of the United Kingdom. A 1978 survey of such estimates put aircraft and large turbogenerators in that category, but found that most of British industry was already sufficiently concentrated to take advantage of such scale economies as were available (DTI 1978, Annex C).

Economies of a different kind can arise from the *learning process* by which managers and operators learn from experience how to use existing facilities and techniques more effectively. It has been suggested that for many industrial products, each doubling of the accumulated volume of production can typically result in a 20 per cent reduction in unit cost, and that this process can continue indefinitely with increases in the length of the production run. In an industry in which learning effects are important, the first manufacturer of a particular product may thus enjoy a cost advantage which subsequent entrants may find difficult to match.

Scale and learning economies have not so far figured in decisions of the European Commission. In Britain they have figured in inquiries by the Monopolies and Mergers Commission in two distinct ways. They have been taken in some cases to indicate that the prospects of entry are likely to be small, and that such prospects are thus unlikely to act as a deterrent to the abuse of market power. In other cases they have been used in the defence of the acquisition of market power – for example, by mergers – to argue that the resulting gains of productive efficiency are the more likely to outweigh any losses of allocative efficiency due to reduced competition.

In a case falling in the first category, the Commission considered that the economies of scale in salt production meant that an entrant would have to capture a substantial share of the UK market in order to avoid operating at a cost disadvantage. In view of the poor prospects of entry and of the weak price competition between the two firms which together supplied 70 per cent of the market, price regulation was recommended (*White Salt 1986*). Comparable scale economies contributed to a similar recommendation in an earlier case involving contraceptive manufacture (*Contraceptive Sheaths 1975*). In face of similar scale economies in the manufacture of flat glass, on the other hand, it was noted that the sole UK supplier had established a very important export trade which it could not maintain unless it were able to exploit to the full the economies of scale which were available to its competitors (*Flat Glass 1968*, par 302).

Quantitative estimates of minimum efficient plant size have been found difficult to make except in relation to the manufacture of a single standardised product. In the case of building bricks it was estimated that a plant producing 250 million fletton bricks per year (about 10 per cent of UK demand) constituted the minimum efficient size, but that in view of high transport costs, it may prove economical to use smaller plants in order to site them nearer to the customer. The operation of plants with lower than the minimum efficient capacity need not, in any case, involve decisive cost penalties since the savings accruing to size increases tend to diminish as the minimum efficient size is approached (*Building Bricks 1976*).

Where the production of a range of different products is commercially important, the concept of minimum efficient size is less clearcut. The minimum efficient size of plant producing a full range of ceramic sanitaryware products was put at 10 000 to 15 000 pieces a week, but it was noted that plants used for a restricted range of products with well below that capacity could be operated at little or no cost disadvantage (*Ceramic Sanitaryware 1978*). Similarly it was found that specialist or local manufacturers of ice cream could operate profitably using small plants but that large-scale production was necessary to compete in the provision of a countrywide supply of a wide range of ice cream products (*Ice Cream 1979*).

E   BRAND LOYALTY AND ADVERTISING

The commonest obstacle to entry is, however, the difficulty of bringing a new product to the attention of potential buyers. Expenditure on capital equipment may be partly recoverable, if entry is unsuccessful, by selling the equipment or putting it to other uses. Promotional expenditure, by contrast, is a sunk cost which cannot be recovered except by successful entry. As has been noted (Section B of Chapter 1) no market in which such sunk costs are important can be regarded as contestable. On the other hand, advertising and other forms of promotion are important as a means of challenging existing market power, and for that reason the authorities have often been reluctant to restrict them. Indeed, artificial restrictions upon advertising imposed by trade associations and professional bodies have generally been condemned as anti-competitive.

Brand Loyalty

Customer loyalty to existing brands has in a number of cases been observed to add to the difficulties of entry. The world-wide use of its 'Chiquita' brand name was held by the European Court to contribute to the dominance of a supplier of bananas (*United Brands 1978*). A proven track record in connection with health and safety on the part of a supplier of food packaging equipment was considered to constitute a barrier to entry (*Tetra Pak/Alpha Laval 1991*). The most extreme form of brand loyalty occurs when customers come to regard a brand as synonymous with the product. In Britain, many domestic purchasers of commercially available butane gas were found to believe that the name of that commodity was 'Calor Gas' – which was one of the reasons for not expecting the dominance of Calor to be seriously eroded in the foreseeable future (*Liquified Petroleum Gas 1981*, par 10.55). Another example was the tendency of doctors to prescribe certain drugs by brand names when identical substances could be obtained at lower cost by using chemical terms (*Librium and Vallium 1973*, par 120).

Historically (e.g., in the case of soap) the benefit of branding to the customer has been its implied guarantee of quality, but over the years that benefit has also been made available for many products by the publication of national quality standards. In one case, a national standard provided an effective substitute: brand loyalty was found to have been virtually eliminated by the requirement that retailers should grade petrol according to its octane rating (*Petrol 1979*). The issue of a British Standard for contraceptives, on the other hand, was found not to have eroded customer loyalty to the Durex brand (*Contraceptive Sheaths 1982*), with the result that entry prospects were considered to remain remote.

Advertising

Advertising has figured in inquiries where it has been sufficiently high to constitute an entry barrier, and where it has been restricted in a way that might hamper entry.

The competition authorities in the EU and in Britain have in several cases taken high levels of advertising as contributory evidence of the existence of market power, but they have generally recognised that advertising is nevertheless a part of the competitive process, and they have seldom sought to limit it. Brand advertising of German dairy products financed by a voluntary levy was found to be contrary to

Article 85(1) (*Milchforderungsfonds 1985*). Advertising expenditures by two dominant soap manufacturers, amounting for each to about 23 per cent of sales, were found by the Monopolies and Mergers Commission to be against the public interest because they displaced price competition, kept newcomers out of the market and raised prices (*Household Detergents 1966*). Potentially harmful effects have been noted in other cases, without implying criticism of the firms concerned. Advertising and promotion expenditures by Kelloggs, at about 13 per cent of sales, were found to have raised prices and to have contributed to the difficulties of entry, but against the background of high levels of advertising in the food industry they were not found to be against the public interest (*Breakfast Cereals 1973*). At 7 per cent of sales, Pedigree's advertising and promotion expenditures on pet foods were not considered unreasonable, but were considered to represent some obstacle to new entrants (*Cat and Dog Foods 1977*). There are signs that the attitudes of the British authorities toward high levels of advertising have changed over the years, and it is to be noted that there have been no adverse public interest findings in that respect during the past 20 years.

While the authorities have thus been reluctant to limit the use of advertising, they have generally sought to remove restrictions upon advertising. In several decisions, the European Commission has stated that such restrictions limit an important aspect of competitive behaviour (for example, *Vimoltu 1983*), and the Commission has advised that cooperation agreements which embody restrictions upon advertising may be regarded as anti-competitive (Commission Notice of 29 July 1968 on cooperation agreements). Under United States law, such restrictions are regarded as an indirect form of price-fixing, and are *per se* illegal. In Britain, agreements to restrict advertising fall outside the scope of the Restrictive Practices Act, but restrictions on advertising have been taken into account in competition and monopoly inquiries. A ban on the advertising of contraceptives was found to have tended to prevent new entrants from challenging the dominance of the Durex brand. Restrictions upon advertising by accountants, veterinary surgeons and solicitors were found to be an obstacle to innovation and to the setting up of new practices and thus to be against the public interest (*Accountancy Services, Veterinary Services, Solicitors' Services 1976*) but barristers' services were found to be in a different category (*Barristers' Services 1976*).

F   INTELLECTUAL PROPERTY RIGHTS

Practices by which firms create entry barriers by means of their pricing and distribution policies – for example predatory pricing and exclusive dealing – are covered in chapters 7 and 8 below. The subject of intellectual property rights is not, however, dealt with elsewhere in this book. That subject will be briefly considered here, and the reader is referred to other works (for example, Whish, 1988, Chapter 7 for British and EU competition law, and Goyder, 1992, Chapters 15 and 16 for Community competition law on the subject) for detailed treatments. EU and British legislation governing intellectual property rights is summarised in section G of Chapter 2, in which it is noted that British law now enables the exercise of such rights to be the subject of references to the Monopolies and Mergers Commission.

The ownership of intellectual property rights has been taken to be contributory evidence of market power, and excessive or unnecessary use of those rights has occasionally been considered to be anti-competitive. In recent years, however, competition authorities have increasingly recognised that patents, copyrights and the like serve the public interest by providing an incentive for innovation which would be lost if the innovator were not given some monopoly rights over his creation (see, for example, OECD, 1989).

A very large number of EU cases were for a time concerned with the use of national patents to restrict imports and thus to impede trade between member countries (summaries of 26 such cases appear in Bellamy and Child, 1987, Chapter 7). The precedents established by those cases are complex, but some straightforward rules can be distinguished. Under a principle known as 'exhaustion of rights', it has been established that a national patent may not be used to prevent imports of a product which the owner of the patent had previously marketed in another member state (*Deutsche Grammophon 1971*). On the other hand a patentee is entitled to exercise patent rights to prevent the import of products sold by a third party in another country where no patent protection is available (*Parke Davis 1968*).

The amassing of patents by a dominant supplier has under certain circumstances been regarded as an anti-competitive practice, designed to prevent entry. The Xerox Group had over a thousand patents and patent applications pertaining to photocopying, had been unwilling to grant licenses, and had opposed the granting of patents to others. Those practices were found to be against the public interest because they had compelled potential competitors to spend a lot of time and money finding the extent of Xerox's patent protection and developing alternatives which were often inferior (*Reprographic Equipment 1976*). The availability of alternatives may, however, be decisive. The ownership by Kodak of ten patents which were of major importance in the manufacture and processing of colour film was held not to constitute an entry barrier because its competitors had been able to develop comparable products by other methods (*Colour Film 1966*).

The unreasonable refusal to grant licences may on its own be considered to constitute an entry barrier, and may be considered anti-competitive. The refusal by the BBC and two others to allow the publication of details of television programmes on which they held copyrights was condemned because its motive was to exclude competition from the market for television guides (*Television Guides 1988 & 1991*). The refusal of a British car manufacturer to grant licences other than to its own suppliers for the manufacture of replacement body parts was found to be against the public interest because it raised the prices of spares, and because motorists would be compelled to scrap older cars if the spares ceased to be available (*Ford 1985*). It was recognised that there was a public interest in the provision of an adequate reward for innovation, but it was considered possible to satisfy that interest and enable the manufacturer to recover its development costs while restricting the period of protection for its designs to five years. That recommendation of the Monopolies and Mergers Commission could not at the time be enforced under existing British copyright law. However, the European Commission, which had also been considering the case, announced in December 1985 that it had obtained an undertaking from Ford that it would offer licences immediately to competitors in the UK for the manufacture and sale of body parts for Ford motor vehicles.

An agreement to license a patent, subject to conditions to be observed by the patentee, could in principle be regarded as a concerted practice or a restrictive trade practice. Having once conceded to the owner of a patent the right to withhold licences, however, there would seem to be little point in preventing him from attaching conditions to those licences which he chooses to grant. In recognition of that logic, Regulation 2349/84 exempts a wide range of bilateral licensing agreements from notification under Article 85(1) of the Treaty of Rome, and Schedule 3 of the Restrictive Trade Practices Act exempts many such agreements from registration under the Act. Exemption from notification under the Treaty is, however, subject to a number of conditions designed to ensure that the restrictions contained in a licensing agreement do not go further than is necessary to further the objective of promoting technical progress. An exclusive licence which fell within the scope of the exempting regulation was nevertheless ruled to be an abuse of a dominant position because it deprived a competitor of the use of new technology (*Tetra Pak 1988 & 1990*). Patent pooling and cross-licensing agreements are not exempted from notification under the Treaty (unless part of certain R&D agreements which are exempted under Regulation 418/85), and pooling agreements involving three or more parties are not excluded from registration under the Restrictive Trade Practices Act.

The European Commission has several times taken action against patent pools (see for example, Comp Rep 11, 1981, p. 62), but no such action appears to have been taken under British law. Action against cross-licensing was considered on one occasion by the Monopolies and Mergers Commission. A manufacturer had agreed to give its dominant competitor the option to obtain non-exclusive licences for up to eight of its patents. The Commission thought it arguable that such an agreement was anti-competitive because it gave the dominant firm the right to take advantage of any technological breakthrough by its main rival, and thus helped to preserve its dominant position. Prohibition of the agreement was not recommended because of its non-exclusive nature, and because of the danger of rendering the dominant British firm more vulnerable to overseas competition (*Postal Franking Machines 1986*).

The treatment of intellectual property rights by the competition authorities has been widely criticised because of the arbitrary fashion in which they have balanced benefits to innovation against detriments to competition. This is a controversial issue on which views have shifted over the years, and on which a settled consensus has yet to be reached.

6 The Control of Mergers and Joint Ventures

A INTRODUCTION

Policy Presumptions

The operation of merger policy depends less upon the enabling legis-lation and its investigatory procedures than upon the presumption which is adopted concerning the general effect of mergers on the public interest. As noted in section C of Chapter 1, a balance has to be struck be-tween expected losses of allocative efficiency resulting from the re-duction of competition and expected gains in productive efficiency; and different authorities may adopt different presumptions in that re-spect. In an early case the European Court of Justice has ruled that an increase in the market share of a dominant undertaking can on its own constitute a breach of the Treaty of Rome (*Continental Can 1973*). European Union merger regulation is not now confined to dominant undertakings, but it does not seek to prevent mergers unless they im-pede *effective competition*. The regulation stipulates that account is to be taken of technical and economic progress which is to the consumers' advantage, but only if no obstacle to competition is created. In prac-tice, however, efficiency gains are often balanced against losses of competition. The commission is, moreover, enjoined to place its appraisal

> within the general framework of the fundamental objectives referred to in Article 2 of the Treaty, including that of strengthening the Community's economic and social cohesion (Rehearsal 13 to Regu-lation 4064/89 examined by the Court of First Instance in *Perrier Union 1992*).

The promotion of competition is only one of the objectives to be sought under British merger legislation. The legislation also requires the promotion of technical progress to be sought *through competition*. But in considering where the public interest lies, those objectives have to be balanced against a number of others, as noted in section A of Chapter 2. British practice is to permit a merger to proceed, even if it

119

leads to a substantial increase in market power, unless there is convincing evidence that it will be against the public interest.

The attitude of the Monopolies and Mergers Commission in that respect is illustrated by statements made in two of their reports. Concerning the proposed merger of Britain's largest sugar merchant with its largest sugar producer, one group commented that:

> The question we have to consider is not merely whether there is a possibility that the merger will operate against the public interest. If only a possibility were required, hardly any merger could be allowed to proceed, for it is very rarely that such a possibility can be quite excluded. The question is whether the merger will operate against the public interest. To put the matter colloquially, the required conclusion is not, 'This may happen' but 'We expect that this will happen'. (*Berisford/British Sugar, 1981*, par 9.40)

In that case the Commission concluded that 'we find no respects in which the merger may be expected to produce clear benefits in relation to the public interest' but the merger was allowed to proceed, subject to certain undertakings. In a later case the investigating group made a similar comment:

> We discern no material advantages to the public interest arising from the proposed merger; but the question before us is whether the merger may be expected to operate against the public interest, and in our view there are not sufficient grounds for such an expectation. (*Scottish & Newcastle/Matthew Brown 1985*, par 7.31)

A 1978 policy review noted that existing policy was biased in favour of mergers, and recommended a move to a more neutral position, but its recommendation was rejected (DTI, 1978). Government policy on the matter was restated in a 1988 White Paper in the following terms:

> The Government believe that there are considerable benefits from allowing freedom for change in corporate ownership and control through mergers and acquisitions. Generally, the market will be a better arbiter than Government of the prospects for the proposed transactions, and will ensure better use of assets, for the benefit of their owners and the economy as a whole. Government should intervene only where the interests of the decision makers in the market are likely to run counter to the public interest. The classic example

of this is where a merger threatens to give the newly-formed enterprise a position of market power which it will be able to exploit at
the expense of its customers. (Cm 279, quoted in full in DTI, 1988,
Annex C)

The benefits from mergers which are referred to in that policy statement are expected to arise from the 'market for corporate control'
According to that theory, management teams compete for the right to
control corporate assets, and management efficiency is ensured by a
natural selection mechanism in which take-overs, or the threat of take-
overs, ensure the survival of the fittest. Poor management performance leads to a weak share price, encouraging a corporate raider to
seize the opportunity to make capital gains by installing a better management team and reaping the benefit in the form of the resulting increase in the share price (Meade, 1968).

The proposition that the threat of a take-over is an effective spur to
managerial efficiency has received some empirical support from a study
of UK mergers (Holl and Pickering, 1986). However, that study and
many others also indicate that mergers do not, on average, lead to
efficiency gains (see DTI 1988, Annex E, and Chiplin and Wright 1987,
Chapter 7 for summaries of such studies).

The Prospects of Abuse

Different policies may also be adopted as to whether to presume that
market power is likely to be abused. The Monopolies and Mergers
Commission have not always adopted that presumption. A merger which
virtually eliminated competition in the supply of mineral insulated cable,
and from which no great economic benefits were expected, was not
opposed by the Commission because of assurances provided by the
acquiring company (*BICC/Pyrotenax 1967*), and in commenting upon
an acquisition which gave Pilkington control of the British safety glass
industry, the group concerned said that:

we do not think that Pilkington is to be criticised for seeking to
control the safety glass industry in this country.... We are satisfied that Pilkington is conscious of its responsibility as a monopolist,
to the public interest ... There would, we think, have to be some
quite unforeseen change in this respect before Pilkington would de-
liberately set out to exploit its position of strength at the expense of
the public interest. (*Flat Glass 1968*)

The European Commission, supported by the European Court of Justice, have taken a different approach. In the leading case which has already been referred to, the argument that in order to bring a merger within the scope of the Treaty of Rome it would be necessary to show some abusive exploitation, as distinct from a mere structural change in the organisation of the two enterprises, was specifically rejected by the Court. (*Continental Can 1973*). The difference in this respect between the EU and UK approaches led the European Commission, in two cases, to impose further or more stringent conditions upon mergers which had been cleared by the Monopolies and Mergers Commission. (*BA/BCal 1987, Minorco/ConsGold 1989*).

B   JURISDICTION AND THE SELECTION OF CASES

The number of mergers which are ruled upon by the competition authorities is very small in proportion to their total incidence. The following sections of this chapter review the treatment by the authorities of some specific issues arising in those merger cases. Of more interest to most businessmen, however, are the characteristics of those mergers which escape regulation, either because they do not fall within its jurisdiction, or because they are excluded by the selection procedures adopted by the authorities.

The European Commission's Jurisdiction

Mergers having a *community dimension* were defined in Regulation 4064/89 as those meeting the following criteria:

(a) the companies concerned have a combined worldwide turnover of at least 5 billion ecu;
(b) at least two of the companies concerned have a Community-wide turnover of at least 250 million ecu;
(c) unless each of the undertakings concerned achieves more than two-thirds of its aggregate Community-wide turnover within one and the same Member State.

The Commission proposes in due course to lower the above thresholds. They are to be reviewed in 1996.

The general intention is that no merger should fall within the jurisdictions both of the Community and of a member state. The European

Commission may, however, refer a qualifying merger to the competition authority of a member state where a problem of market dominance arises in a distinct market within that member state, which is isolated from the rest of the Community, for example, by high transport costs.

The Commission referred a merger involving Tarmac and Steetley to the UK authorities at their request, although it satisfied the criteria for EU jurisdiction, because it would have given the combined firm control of almost 80 per cent of brickmaking capacity in the northwest of England. (That merger would have had no effects outside the UK, however, despite Steetley's large French interests.)

In exceptional circumstances a member country may be able to exclude a qualifying merger from the Commission's jurisdiction. The application of the regulation is stated to be without prejudice to Article 223 of the Treaty and not to prevent member states from taking appropriate measures to protect legitimate interests other than those pursued by the regulation. (Rehearsal 28 and Article 21(3) of Regulation 4064/89). The UK government considered British Aerospace's 1994 bid for VSEL to fall within that category because it affected national security interests, and instructed British Aerospace not to notify the bid to the Commission. That contention was accepted by the European Commission as regards the military aspects of the merger, but its non-military aspects were examined and cleared, following the Commission's normal merger procedures. The Commission indicated, however, that exemption from notification in respect even of military activities would not have been accepted had there been more than slight effects in other member states (Comp Rep 1994, p. 219).

United Kingdom Merger Jurisdiction

As noted in section F of chapter 2, a merger situation qualifying for investigation is taken to occur under UK law if two or more enterprises cease to be distinct enterprises, at least one of which was carried on in the UK, and if either their combined market share exceeds 25 per cent, or the value of the assets taken over exceeds £70 million. British mergers jurisdiction is limited, however by the rule that

> no member state shall apply its national legislation on competition to any consideration that has a Community dimension. (Article 21(2) Regulation 4064/89)

Although no merger should fall within both jurisdictions, questions of definition may create some uncertainty as to which jurisdiction is to prevail. The Director-General of Fair Trading has advised companies who are in doubt to notify both authorities in order to avoid delay. (Letter to the *Financial Times* 25 October 1990)

The Scope of the Definition of a Merger

Jurisdiction is not confined to mergers in which more than 50 per cent of a company's shares are acquired. It is sufficient under British law that there should be an ability to exert a *material influence* upon policy. The Office of Fair Trading advise that:

A shareholding of more than 25 per cent, which generally enables the holder to block special resolutions, is likely to be regarded as conferring the ability to influence policy even if all the remaining shares are held by one person. Any shareholding greater than 15 per cent is liable to be examined to see whether or not the holder may be able materially to influence the policy of the company concerned, though a holding of less than 15 per cent might also attract scrutiny in exceptional circumstances. (OFT guides Mergers 1991 page 4)

The ability to influence policy by means of a successful threat to withdraw support was considered to confer material influence in a case involving the acquisition of a 20 per cent shareholding (*Stagecoach/ Mainline 1995*).

Also, a transfer of assets may be deemed to constitute a qualifying merger, even if the business concerned is not transferred to the acquiring firm as a going concern. Because of the continued operation of bus services from an acquired depot, that acquisition was considered to qualify although it would have been possible – though not commercially sensible – to operate the services without the depot. (*Stagecoach/ Lancaster City 1993*)

Under EU merger law, control is deemed to be constituted by:

rights or contracts which confer decisive influence on the composition, voting or decisions of the organs of an undertaking. (Article 3(3) of the merger regulation)

In one case a 19 per cent holding combined with a right to appoint the chairman and the chief executive was held to constitute control (*CCIE/ GTE 1992*).

Also, in the case of joint ventures, control may be conferred by contracts concerning the running of the business (Commission Notice OJ C 203 of 14/8/1990). The possibility of joint control is recognised when there are equal shareholdings or when joint consent is required for important decisions.

The Criteria for Selection

As has been noted, all mergers having a *community dimension* (as defined above) must be notified to the European Commission. More than three-quarters of those notified are cleared within a month under Article 6.1(b) of the mergers regulation as not raising serious doubts as to their compatibility with the Common Market. There is a presumption that a merger leading to a combined market share of less than 25 per cent will be cleared under that procedure (rehearsal 15 to the merger regulation).

Under British legislation there is no requirement to notify a merger to the Office of Fair Trading, although as noted in section C of Chapter 3, it may save time to do so. As noted there, about 3 per cent of the mergers examined by the Office are referred to the Monopolies and Mergers Commission by the Secretary of State on the advice of the Director-General of Fair Trading. The considerations governing selection are stated in general terms in the OFT mergers guide, and some further broad indications can be gleaned from the record.

The mergers guidelines issued by the Office of Fair Trading contain no numerical criteria for the selection of mergers for reference to the Monopolies and Mergers Commission, but it may be assumed that combined market share is often an important consideration. The fact that a 25 per cent market share constitutes one of the alternative criteria for reference does not, however, mean that mergers leading to lower market shares cannot be referred. Where – as discussed below – references are made on grounds other than their effect upon competition, mergers involving no increase in market share may, of course, be included, as is also the case where vertical integration is at issue.

Mergers in distribution leading to very small national market shares have been referred in cases where there would nevertheless be substantial market shares in particular localities. In food retailing, a merger leading to a national market share of only 4 per cent was referred, and although the Monopolies and Mergers Commission did not detect any local market share above 10 per cent, that was probably because of their practice of calculating market shares for television areas rather than for shopping areas (*Linfood/Fitch Lovell 1983*). A merger which has no implications for national market share may also be referred if it is likely to produce a dominant position in a world market (*Minorco/Consolidated Gold Fields 1989*). In some other cases, the market shares which had been considered in deciding to make the reference may have differed from those which the Commission subsequently considered to be relevant to their inquiries. Otherwise, there have been no references on competition grounds of horizontal mergers leading to a combined market share of less than 25 per cent.

It may reasonably be concluded that, in the absence of special factors of the sort which have been discussed above, a merger which leads to a combined market share which is less than 25 per cent is unlikely to be referred. It cannot, however, be concluded that all qualifying mergers leading to market shares substantially in excess of 25 per cent are likely to be referred. The mitigating factors referred to in Chapter 5, which can affect the interpretation of market share statistics, may sometimes be decisive. As noted in section B of that chapter, a merger producing a 94 per cent share of the British market for automotive bearings was not referred, despite the absence of import penetration, because it was considered that purchasers could readily obtain their supplies from elsewhere in Europe. Even in the absence of such mitigating factors, a merger leading to a combined market share well in excess of 25 per cent may still escape reference if it strengthens the ability of firms in the 'second division' to compete with the dominant market leaders. Such might, for example, have been the reason for not referring the supermarket mergers of Argyll with Safeway and of Dee with Fine Fare.

It is normally to be expected that any merger involving major companies in a highly concentrated market would be referred to the Commission. Some uncertainty has, however, been introduced on that point by the unexplained rejection in 1993 by the then Secretary of State of the Director-General's advice to refer Airtours' bid for Owners Abroad as a result of which control over two thirds of the market was obtained.

Non-competition References

Section E below reviews the treatment by the Monopolies and Mergers Commission of various non-competition issues which have arisen in merger cases. In many of the cases considered, such issues had in fact constituted the principal reason for making the reference. A change in the emphasis of policy toward such references was, however, announced in 1984 when Mr Norman Tebbit, the then Secretary of State for Trade and Industry, said:

> my policy has been and will continue to be to make references primarily on competition grounds. (House of Commons written answer, 5 July 1984)

It is to be noted, however, that the new policy did not exclude references on non-competition grounds, nor did it require that all mergers raising competition issues would referred. Subsequent policy statements have maintained substantially the same position. A later Secretary of State said about merger references that:

> the main, though not exclusive, consideration should be their potential effect on competition. (Speech by Lord Young, 8 October 1987)

A rare exception may occur when there are rival bids, not all of which raise competition issues. There has been thought to be an equity argument under those circumstances for referring all of the bids. That was not done in 1993 when Lloyds Bank and the Hong Kong and Shanghai Bank made bids for Midland Bank. Only the Lloyds bid was referred, as a result of which the rival bid went through uncontested. It was done in 1994 when the General Electric Company and British Aerospace both bid for the submarine-maker VSEL. Both bids were referred although the British Aerospace bid raised no competition issues. It would not make sense to refer a bid which raised no public interest issues, however, and unspecified non-competition issues were given as the reason for referring the British Aerospace bid.

Among the non-competition issues on which subsequent references have been based are the matters of highly leveraged bids, national security and acquisitions by state-controlled firms. Nevertheless it seems likely that in the foreseeable future there will be few departures from the 'Tebbit Doctrine' referred to.

C   THE TREATMENT OF HORIZONTAL MERGERS

In the absence of mitigating factors, there is a reasonable presumption that mergers which lead to a combined market share greater than about 40 per cent will be found to be against the public interest. Of some 50 mergers in that category which have been reported on by the Monopolies

TABLE 2   *Some horizontal mergers with combined market share greater than 40% which were not opposed*

Merger	Combined market share %	Principal reason
UK cases		
a *British Rail/Hoverlloyd 1981*	100	Rationalisation
b *Happy Eater/Little Chef 1987*	93*	Substitutes
c *Hillsdown/Ass British Foods 1992*	90	Rationalisation
d *Strong & Fisher/Pittard Garnar 1989*	87	Entry prospects
e *Monsanto/Rhone-Poulenc 1989*	86	World market
f *Swedish Match/Alleghany 1987*	82	Jobs/conduct
g *BA/BCal 1987*	75	Conduct
h *Trafalgar House/P&O 1984*	72	Entry prospects
i *Gillette/Parker Pen 1993*	72	Entry prospects
j *Prosper de Mulder/Croda 1991*	65	Low share increase
k *Tiphook/Trailerent 1990*	65	Substitutes
l *Glynwed/Lees 1989*	63	Entry prospects
m *Nabisco/Huntley & Palmer 1982*	60*	2nd best/jobs
n *Trellebourg/McKechnie 1990*	52	imports
o *P&O/European Ferries 1986*	50	Entry prospects
p *Norton Opax/McCorquodale 1986*	49	Buying power
q *Dee/Booker McConnell 1985*	48	2nd best/conduct
r *London Brick/Ibstock Johnson 1983*	48*	Conduct
s *BET/SGB 1986*	46	Entry prospects
t *Hillsdown/Pittard/Garnar 1989*	44	imports
EU Cases		
A *Alcatel/Telettra 1991*	83	Buying power
B *Courtaulds/SNIA 1991*	65	import prospects
C *ABB/BREL 1992*	50	Strong competitor
D *Air France/Sabena 1992*	50	Entry prospects
E *Varta/Bosch 1991*	44	New entry

and Mergers Commission over a recent 15-year period, more than half have nevertheless been cleared. Some of the mergers in question are listed in Table 2 together with five European Commission cases falling within the same category. (The market shares quoted in that table are the highest reported in each case, and those marked with an asterisk differ from those which were considered relevant by the Commission. Also, as explained below, the reasons cited were seldom the only reasons for permitting the merger.)

Market Characteristics: Concentration and Competition

The major influence upon the treatment of mergers has been the extent of effective competition to be expected in the affected markets. The European Commission is required to take account of that prospect and of the market position of the firms concerned. In highly concentrated markets, mergers leading to market shares well below 40 per cent have normally been prohibited by both the UK and the EU authorities. In the context of the concentrated and vertically integrated UK beer market, for example, a market share limit of 15 per cent has been proposed – although not implemented (*Elders/Grand Met 1990*).

In many of the cases listed in Table 2, however, adequate effective competition was expected to survive despite the creation of high combined market shares. Even in concentrated markets, the presence of a strong and active competitor was decisive in case *c* and the *second best* argument (discussed below) was influential in cases *m* and *q*. The quoted market shares were believed to understate competitive pressures because of availability of *substitutes* (as discussed in section B of Chapter 5) in cases *b* and *k*, and because of import penetrations (of 14, 18 and 35 per cent) in cases *e*, *n* and *t*. The influence of potential imports and other *entry prospects* (discussed in detail in section C of Chapter 5) were important influences upon the decisions taken in cases *d*, *h*, *i*, *l*, *o*, *s* & *t* and in cases *B* and *D*, and the anticipated effects of a new entry tipped the balance in case *E*. The countervailing *power of buyers* (see Section A of Chapter 5) was decisive in cases *A* and *p*.

The authorities have taken a more permissive attitude toward high market shares in markets characterised by vigorous competition even where there are high levels of concentration (as in case *j*). A merger which raised the already high level of concentration in the market for recorded music was cleared because there was vigorous competition in that market, although by promotion rather than by relative prices. (*Thorn EMI/Virgin 1992*). And the European Commission have stated that high market shares in high-growth markets involving modern technology do not, in any case, necessarily indicate undesirable market power (*Digital/Phillips 1991*).

Rationalisation

There have been some cases where it has been argued that mergers leading to high market shares confer a net benefit by enabling excess capacity to be removed. The Commission have made the following statement concerning the formation of *crisis cartels*:

> The Commission may be able to condone agreements in restraint of competition which relate to a sector as a whole, provided that they are aimed solely at achieving a coordinated reduction of over-capacity, do not otherwise restrict decision-making by the firms involved. The necessary structural reorganisation must not be achieved by unsuitable means such as price-fixing or quota agreements . . . The Commission must be satisfied that after the reorganisation is complete there will still be a sufficient number of Community manufacturers left to maintain effective competition. (Comp Rep 23 1993)

The existence of overcapacity in the Dutch building brick industry led the Commission to approve an agreement among 16 producers to close seven plants but otherwise not to restrict competition (Commission press release IP/94/353 of 2/5/94).

In the UK there have been several cases in which it has been argued that the merger would contribute to economic progress by eliminating excess capacity or by rescuing a firm that could not otherwise survive.

That argument was accepted in case *a* of Table 2. Both companies had suffered losses in the face of strong price competition and it seemed possible that they might cease hovercraft operations if the merger were not permitted, removing hovercraft competition with other services. (Clearance for that merger was, however, made subject to statutory undertakings, as noted below.) Rationalisation was also an issue in case *o*. The Commission saw prospects of some degree of rationalisation without the merger but thought that the merger would facilitate other rationalisation measures which would otherwise be against the interests of the separate companies; and in view of good entry prospects, it found the merger not to be against the public interest. In case c, the merger was held not to result in a loss of competition because the raspberry operations of Associated British Foods would have been closed if the merger had not taken place.

In an earlier case involving European Ferries, however, the Commission was not convinced that a merger which would have yielded a combined market share of 71 per cent was either the best or the only way to deal with the ferry industry's problems of excess capacity. It was noted at that time that entry which had occurred over the previous decade had not prevented prices from rising, and European Ferries were considered to be in a position to counter further attempts at entry by obstructing access to ports. The Commission concluded that, even if it were the case that the merger provided the solution to current difficulties, it would in any event be unacceptable because of the resulting market share, which would be expected to lead to higher prices and a reduction of choice (*European Ferries/Sealink 1981*). Nor was the need for rationalisation of the refractories industry accepted as sufficient justification for a merger of two companies in that industry whose market shares totalled 67 per cent. The Commission expected at least one major producer to survive without the merger, and feared that if it took place, customers who wished to have more than one source of supply would turn to foreign suppliers, which it thought would be against the public interest because of the adverse effect on employment (*Hepworth/Steetley 1984*).

Employment

As noted in section A of Chapter 2, the objectives embodied in the public interest criterion of the Fair Trading Act include that of 'promoting the balanced distribution of industry and employment'. In fact, employment considerations have seldom figured significantly in merger cases.

The preservation of employment in a situation of excess capacity was, however, the main consideration in case f of Table 2. The Commission's conclusion in that case reads:

> This is a merger which would lead to a substantial degree of additional concentration in an already highly concentrated market. We believe, however that, in the exceptional circumstances of the declining market which we have described, it is unlikely that a merged Bryant & May/Masters would raise prices unreasonably, or materially reduce the number of brands available, or the standards of service to customers. We believe that this merger would provide a greater degree of job security at Bryant & May's Liverpool factory and would secure a continuation of match making in the United Kingdom for a longer period than would otherwise be the case.

Employment was also a consideration in case m, the report of which concluded that:

> while the outlook for employment in HPF is not good, it is not likely to become materially worse, and may in the long run become better if the merger takes place.

In that case, however, the Commission's judgement was that the merger would in any case benefit competition because of the greater strength of the merged companies to compete with the dominant biscuit manufacturer, United Biscuits. (The merged company would have a 24 per cent share of that market as against United Biscuits' 40 per cent and, as noted in section B of Chapter 5, the Commission did not consider their 60 per cent share of the market for plain biscuits to be relevant.) The argument that a merger would result in a loss of employment was rejected in *Perrier Union 1992* but the possibility of taking that consideration into account under EU merger law was not ruled out.

The Second Best

The argument used in case m that, given the existence of a dominant firm, competition is enhanced by a merger between two of its smaller competitors has also been accepted in connection with supermarket groups. That argument may, as has been suggested in the previous section of this chapter, have been the reason for not referring some such mergers. It was accepted in the case of a merger which was to create the largest United Kingdom food group with both wholesaling and retailing interests (*Linfood/Fitch Lovell 1983*), and in the further merger involving Linfood (renamed Dee) listed as case *q* in Table 2. It was rejected, however, in the case of a proposed merger of two brewers which would have given them a combined market share comparable with that of the market leader, at about 40 per cent (*Elders/ Scottish & Newcastle 1989*). The Commission considered that in that case there was no guarantee that two such large companies would compete effectively, and that on the contrary they might seek to avoid direct competition and adopt practices which would increase the difficulties of others in competing.

Business Conduct

It was noted in section A of this chapter that the Monopolies and Mergers Commission has in some cases (such as those concerning Bryant and May, BICC and Pilkington) not taken an unfavourable view of the acquisition of a substantial degree of market power because it considered it unlikely that the power would be abused.

In case *g*, the Commission took account of (legally unenforceable) undertakings given to them by British Airways – a practice which, as noted in section G of Chapter 3, was unsuccessfully challenged in the courts. In case *q*, the Commission thought that the threat of entry would prevent Dee from increasing its wholesale prices in areas where competition is weak, that it would be unlikely to use predatory pricing tactics to prevent entry in those areas, and that it would be against their interests to exploit the independent retailers who were their main customers. In case *r*, the Commission felt unable to conclude that the merged company may be expected to prejudice the public interest by exploitation of its market power in view of its past record as total monopolist in the supply of fletton bricks, and in view of the companies' arguments that it would be against their commercial interest to do so.

In the case of a merger between two major music publishers (which had vertical as well as horizontal implications) the Commission concluded that:

> while the possibility remains of Warner/Chappell misusing such market power as it will possess as the result of the merger, the evidence given to us falls short of establishing the expectation that it will in fact behave in such a way. Moreover, even if Warner/Chappell were to do so in the future, there may well be legal remedies available, both through the courts and through action taken by competition authorities. (*Warner/Chappell 1988*)

The availability of remedies under competition legislation was also cited as a reason for discounting the prospects of abuse in the Europcar case referred to in the next section.

Where the acquiring company is merely increasing its holding in a company which it already controls, there is a presumption that business conduct will not change (*BET/Initial 1985*).

Statutory Undertakings

Negotiations before formal notification often enable proposals to be cleared after the removal of features considered objectionable by DGIV officials. Also, under Article 8.2 of Regulation 4064/89 a merger proposal may be modified after notification by undertakings volunteered by the companies (or imposed upon them in cases where the merger has already taken place) in order to make them acceptable.

In the UK, as noted in section C of Chapter 3, the Companies Act 1989 enables the Secretary of State to accept undertakings on divestment from parties to a merger instead of referring the merger to the Commission, and the Deregulation and Contracting Out Act 1994 includes provisions to extend this to other types of undertakings, such as those concerning behaviour. Divestment undertakings have been successfully used for that purpose in connection with the mergers involving Rank/ Mecca, Hillsdown/Strong & Fisher, International Marine/Benjamin Priest, Williams Holdings/Racal and Trafalgar House/Davey.

Some of the reports of the Monopolies and Mergers Commission contain references to undertakings given to it in the course of its inquiries (e.g., in case *g* above). These are not legally binding, and are to be distinguished from statutory undertakings subsequently given to the Director-General of Fair Trading following a recommendation by the Commission. Under Section 88 of the Fair Trading Act the Director-General is required to monitor compliance with such statutory undertakings. If he finds himself in doubt concerning compliance, he may advise the Secretary of State to enforce the undertaking by means of a legally binding statutory order.

The offer of a statutory undertaking may lead the Commission to clear the merger on condition that the undertaking is given. In case *a* above, for example, clearance was made subject to the renewal of an undertaking not to agree car ferry fares with other operators. Alternatively, the merger as it stands may be found to be against the public interest, but action to remedy its adverse effects – which may take the form of a statutory undertaking – may be recommended (*Berisford/ British Sugar 1981*, *BT/Mitel 1986*, *GEC-Siemens/Plessey 1989*). It was concluded that the adverse public interest consequences of the merger of two book clubs with a combined market share of 70 per cent could be remedied by a satisfactory modification of an exclusive dealing 'Concordat' (*Book Club Associates/Leisure Circle 1988*). The remedy may have the effect of preventing the parties from putting some aspects of the merger into effect while allowing others to proceed. A 1988 report recommended the disposal of some local funeral services, the acquisition of which had produced market shares of between 77 and 100 per cent, while allowing others, giving market shares of 64 per cent and less, to be retained (*CWS/House of Fraser 1987*). The divestment of those advertising sites in areas in which the market share of the acquiring company exceeded 25 per cent was recommended in another case (*MAI/Continental 1987*).

D VERTICAL AND CONGLOMERATE MERGERS

Vertical Issues

The merger of a dominant firm with one of its suppliers raises the possibility that it may manipulate its 'upstream' market to the detriment of its competitors. It is unlikely to be able to do so, however, unless it acquires a substantial share of that market. The market share acquired has been found to be too small to endanger competition in a number of cases examined by the European Commission (such as *AT&T/NCR 1991* and *Mitsubishi/UCAR 1991*). In the UK, permission for a telephone company to acquire a telephone manufacturer was made subject to a statutory undertaking limiting the UK market share of the equipment (*BT/Mitel 1986*). And the acquisition of Britain's largest sugar refiner by its largest sugar merchant was made subject to the cessation by the merchant of trading in sugar from a competing refiner and the maintenance of the refiner as a separate subsidiary with its own accounts (*Berisford/British Sugar 1981*).

It is similarly possible that the 'downstream' acquisition of a sales outlet could be used to restrict competition – but with the same qualification concerning downstream market share. The merger of a packaging company with an aluminium company was permitted by the European Commission because 40 per cent of the packaging market was met by other suppliers and there were other vertically-integrated aluminium companies in that market (*Viag/Continental Can 1991*). Similarly, the acquisition of a distributor by a steel producer was cleared because a sufficient number of independent distributors remained (*ASD/Usinor 1991*). The Monopolies and Mergers Commission cleared a merger between two car rental firms in one of which a car manufacturer had an interest, on the basis of assurances that the manufacturer's cars would not be supplied to it on preferential terms (*Europcar/Godfrey Davis 1981*).

Conglomerate Mergers

Mergers can sometimes raise competition issues even when there is no apparent horizontal or vertical integration. The Monopolies and Mergers Commission have referred to the dangers of cross-subsidisation and the loss of financial information (*Blue Circle/Armitage Shanks 1980*) but have yet to block a conglomerate merger. Where the merging firms produce complementary products, there is a further risk that they may

restrict competition by marketing their products together as an integrated system. That possibility has been examined but rejected in several cases considered by the European Commission (e.g. *Matsushita/
MCA 1991* and *Tetra Pak/Alpha Laval 1991*).

E NON-COMPETITION ISSUES

In effects-based systems such as those adopted by the Community and
by the United Kingdom, the implementation of merger policy requires
the balancing of the consequences of a merger for competition against
other consequences bearing upon the public interest. As has been noted,
the concept of the public interest underlying British competition policy
is so broad that scarely any consequence of a merger is necessarily
excluded. A special feature of British merger policy has, however, been
the number of cases in which non-competition issues have predominated.

Managerial Conflict and Performance

Hostile bids, in particular, can raise the question for shareholders whether
the new management would be able to command the loyalty of employees and conduct business effectively. In one or two cases involving well-known companies, that question has been put to the Monopolies
and Mergers Commission. It was repeatedly addressed in the course of
inquiries into a series of bids involving the Harrods department store
and the Lonrho conglomerate. The bids raised no competition issues,
and the management style of Lonrho's chairman was the central issue
throughout. In the first and third of those cases it was concluded that
the risk of managerial conflict was not sufficient to warrant an adverse
public interest finding, (*Lonrho/Suits 1979*, *Lonrho/House of Fraser
1985*) but in the second case that risk was considered to justify prohibiting the merger. (*Lonrho/House of Fraser 1981*). In response to
complaints that Lonrho had used unacceptable tactics in an attempt to
disrupt the House of Fraser's management, the Commission stated that:

> Corporate behaviour is regulated by the Companies Act and other
> statutes. It is also subject to the regulations of the Stock Exchange
> and the City Code on Takeovers and Mergers. It has not been
> suggested to us that Lonrho's conduct in the course of its relations
> with the House of Fraser has involved the breach of any statute or
> any of these rules. Conduct which does not amount to any such

breach is of no relevance to the Commission's findings in the absence of specific effects (for example on competition or employment) on the public interest. Conduct which does not infringe the law or other rule may be found offensive or undesirable by some people, but unless such specific effects can be identified it cannot provide a reason for concluding that a merger may be expected to operate against the public interest. (*Lonrho/House of Fraser 1985*)

Since that case, there have been no references concerned solely with the management styles of bidders; and further references of that sort are unlikely. Two cases in which the questions at issue were the conduct and integrity of the bidders had in fact been referred since 1979. The acquisition of the auctioneers Sothebys by an American businessman – considered by the Commission to be successful and highly reputable – was found not to be against the public interest (*Taubman/Sotheby 1983*). About another businessman whose record had included successes and failures – some of which had left creditors unpaid – the Commission concluded that neither his successes nor his failures had, as far as their investigations had gone, been shown to require it to find his merger proposal against the public interest (*Lewis/Illingworth Morris 1983*).

Even if no further cases are referred solely on the above grounds, the question of future management performance is likely to arise in cases referred mainly on other grounds. Disputes between the managements of the bidding and the target company as to which of them could perform better, are of course, a commonplace feature of contested bids. The claim that the target company had not been efficiently managed, and that left to itself it would fail to achieve adequate returns was rejected as justification for a merger which would substantially reduce competition in the cabinet towel rental market in the following terms:

the general direction in which the business of Johnson is likely to go is not in itself a matter which concerns the public interest. The public interest would be involved if we took the view that Johnson was unlikely ever to be more than a negligible competitor in the rental field, in which case its elimination as a competitor would be of little consequence . . . We do not take this view. Thus, although there may well be argument as to the most appropriate form of organisation for Johnson, this is a matter which by itself does not affect the public interest, and on which we do not need to reach any conclusion. (*Sunlight/Initial/Johnson 1983*)

In the above case, the Commission accepted that the proposed merger would lead to friction and disruption arising from changes in organisation and management style and from the negation of deeply held views on the proper way to manage the business, but did not refer to those considerations in summing up the case against the merger. In the case of the proposed takeover of a small Scottish whisky distiller by a large multinational distiller, on the other hand, the Commission attached a good deal of importance to the possibility of a loss of efficiency resulting from management conflicts. The Commission noted that, apart from the bad feelings that might arise over a contested merger, there were strongly held differences concerning the technique of whisky production and about the merits of exporting malt whisky in bulk. It was concluded that relationships after the merger were unlikely to be easy and that the public interest would suffer as the result of the adverse effects this would have on the efficiency of the business, as well as from the reduction in competition (*Hiram Walker/Highland 1980*). Possible management conflicts over employee participation were a consideration in prohibiting a bus company merger. The Commission observed that

The cultures of the two companies are so different as to be incompatible in the longer run. (*Stagecoach/Mainline 1995*)

In conglomerate merger cases, attention may be given to the management problems which can arise from the bidder's lack of experience in the activities of the target company. In the case of a bid for a British process plant and engineering construction business by an American oil exploration and construction company, the Commission doubted whether the bidder could contribute much to the target company's technological or project management expertise. They were concerned that there would be some disturbance and possible loss of efficiency as the new owner was learning about the business which it acquired, and the existing management were learning to work under a new system of control. The merger was found to be against the public interest, partly on those grounds and because of the lengthening of the chain of managerial control, but also because of the detriments to exports and employment which were expected to arise from the loss of Davy's national character and of its position as a British bidder in international markets (*Enserch/Davy 1981*).

Gearing

The Commission's statement about the Sunlight/Johnson merger quoted above suggests that in some cases there may not be a hard-and-fast distinction between competition and non-competition issues. If some non-competition effect of the merger (in that case, improved management performance) could determine whether a supplier is likely to survive as an effective competitor in a market, then that effect may have indirect consequences for competition. Similar indirect consequences could arise if a highly-leveraged bid created the risk of the subsequent financial collapse of the merged organisation. In a later case the Commission rejected the view that market forces can always be relied upon to repair the loss of a major competitor in this way without damage to the public interest:

> there is a view that even if the merged group were to be so extended financially that it collapsed, the normal operation of market forces would ensure the most effective allocation of resources. Buyers would come forward for the businesses that were viable, and other suppliers would step in to meet the demand for the goods and services previously supplied by those that were not. Natural selection would have ensured the survival of the fittest.
>
> We recognise that this argument might be applicable in some cases, although there is inevitably a cost involved in both financial and human terms that may be considerable and ought not to be ignored. However, when dealing with a company of the size and importance of Allied-Lyons, account must be taken of possible detrimental effects on the public interest if the company were to become financially over-extended. In this case these might include the weakening of a major competitor in the national brewing industry, which could lead to damage to its suppliers and customers, to substantial disruption to trade and industry, job losses on a serious scale, and the possible loss to the United Kingdom of markets – including the home market – to overseas suppliers. (*Elders/Allied-Lyons 1986*)

The Commission took account of Elders' history of expansion by successful acquisition, noting that at one stage in that process it had raised its gearing ratio to no less than 530 per cent. In view of its size, the efficiency of its management, and the fact that its target was a mature company with a stable cash flow, the Commission did not think that the merger would result in such financial stringency as would prejudice the development of Allied-Lyons. In a subsequent case involving Elders, the Commission took a similar view of a level of gearing which could – depending on the method of calculation – be as high as 277 per cent (*Elders/Scottish & Newcastle 1989*).

Gearing has not been a significant issue in any inquiry since 1989.

State-controlled Companies

In July 1990, the then Secretary of State for Trade and Industry announced his intention of paying close attention to the degree of state control, if any, of an acquiring company in deciding whether to make a merger reference. He referred to the danger of 'nationalisation by the back door' and to the misallocation of resources to be expected because of state-controlled companies' immunity from market forces. The Commission's response was that they could not accept any general presumption against acquisitions by state-controlled companies, but that the weight to be attached to the effect of state control would have to depend on an evaluation of all the evidence, against the background of the circumstances of the case in question. (*Kemira/ICI 1991*) In June 1991, after the Commission had cleared four acquisitions by foreign state-controlled companies, the Secretary of State indicated that in the absence of sound reasons for referring a merger on competition grounds, state control on its own would no longer be regarded as a good enough reason for a reference.

F   JOINT VENTURES

Some joint ventures are treated by the regulatory authorities in the same way as mergers, and others are treated as restrictive practices. In the terminology of the European Union, the former are termed *concentrative*, and the latter *cooperative*. As has been noted in section F of Chapter 2 that distinction is explained in detail in a Commission Notice (OJ C 203 14/8/1990). Broadly speaking, a joint venture is considered to be cooperative if it is a temporary arrangement, or if it is *partially-functioning* (if, for example, it supplies the product only to the parent companies) or if it is *fully-functioning* but its purpose is to coordinate the competitive behaviour of its parents. Concentrative joint ventures are subject to the merger regulation (4064/89) as described above, and cooperative joint ventures which restrict competition are regulated by Article 85(1) of the Treaty and its relevant block exemptions.

The Commission has stated that it takes a basically favourable attitude to cooperative joint ventures, provided that they:

> make economic sense, do not impose disproportionate restrictions on the undertakings concerned and do not jeopardise the maintenance or development of effective competition. (Comp Rep 22, 1992 p. 171)

Exemptions from Article 85

If the parents are not actual or potential competitors and do not operate in the same market as the joint venture, competition is deemed not to be restricted and the prohibition in Article 85 does not apply. In many other cases, exemption from that prohibition is obtainable. The size of the combined market share of the parents is a major consideration affecting the granting of exemptions. Article 85 does not apply where that share is less than 5 per cent, a fully-functioning joint venture is deemed to be generally acceptable if it does not exceed 10 per cent, and there is a presumption in favour of partially-functioning joint ventures whose parents' market share does not total more than 20 per cent.

Block exemptions are available, as noted below, for certain specialisation and Research and Development (R&D) agreements. Individual exemption of other joint venture agreements is often granted by the Commission. The Commission has stated, however, that exemption will be granted only where there is expected to be an efficiency gain in which consumers will get a fair share, where the only restrictions are those which are indispensable to that objective, and where the arrangement does not enable competition to be eliminated to any substantial extent (Commission Notice OJ C43 16/2/1993). The Commission warns that sales joint ventures are unlikely to be exempted except when they are a necessary feature of a broader arrangement, and that purchasing joint ventures will not normally be exempted.

The specialisation regulation (No 417/85) sets out in detail the conditions under which exemption applies automatically to arrangements under which several firms leave the manufacture of particular products to a joint venture set up by them. The parents' combined turnover must not exceed ECU 1,000 million (except if the agreement is notified and the Commission raises no objection within six months), the total of their market shares must be within the limits referred to above, and there must be no undue restrictions upon supply or distribution. Regulation No 418/85 similarly exempts specified categories of joint

R&D agreement, subject to the same market share limits, but with no turnover limit. Restrictions are permitted on manufacture and patent licensing, but not on sales.

The first arrangement which the Commission exempted as a cooperative joint venture was one in which research and development into active matrix liquid crystal displays was undertaken on behalf of three major electronics companies (*Phillips/Thomson/Sagem 1993*).

Exemptions From Court Proceedings Under the Restrictive Practices Act 1976

The Office of Fair Trading has issued the following broad guidelines concerning the grounds on which it may seek an order (as described in section C of Chapter 3) not to take court proceedings against joint ventures under the Restrictive Trade Practices Act:

> Joint ventures commonly include restrictions on the parent companies not to compete with the joint venture. In considering such restrictions the Office looks for clear evidence of competition in the relevant market from other suppliers or from other substitute goods or services and that no evidence of possible detriments to third parties has been forthcoming. A number of such joint venture agreements which in their original form were thought to contain significant restrictions have been modified to make them suitable for a representation to the Secretary of State. Joint venture agreements to promote research and development may also be suitable for a representation if the Office is satisfied that, without the restrictions they contain, the development would not take place. (OFT guides, Restrictive Practices)

7 Pricing Policies

A INTRODUCTION

While many of the commercial policies which are adopted by businesses may be pursued under conditions of secrecy, their pricing policies are necessarily open to inspection and analysis. It would seem that analysis of those policies offers the best prospect of detecting departures from competitive market conditions, and that their regulation should provide one of the most effective ways of limiting any resulting damage to the public interest. As this chapter will show, those appearances are deceptive. In fact, the treatment of pricing policies has often faced the competition authorities with some of their most serious conceptual, analytical and practical problems.

The conceptual difficulties stem from the limitations of available competition theory. The propositions of 'mainstream' competition theory (the assumptions of which were summarised in section B of Chapter 1) lead to straightforward rules as to what constitutes competitive pricing. But it is in this connection that the simplifications adopted by that theory are most apt to appear unrealistic. Rules which are derived for the pricing of risklessly developed undifferentiated products can hardly be expected to apply at all widely to today's markets. Alternative theories which are based upon more realistic assumptions indicate that economic efficiency could often be increased by departures from those rules, but those theories do not yield an alternative set of rules.

The analytical and practical aspects of the problems have at times led the authorities to make prolific use of specialist terminology, acronyms and abbreviations from the fields of finance, accounting and economics. Terms shown in italics in this chapter are explained in Annex 7.1 Also, in the interests of clarity, acronyms have been replaced by words in quotations from the Commission's reports.

Innovation

The conceptual problems of making a public interest judgement about pricing policies are among their most acute in the context of innovation. Under the simplified assumptions of mainstream competition theory, a profit-maximising business which is operating under fully competi-

143

tive conditions must set the price of each of its products equal to the *marginal cost* of supplying it. Conversely, a business which is able to set the price of any product above that level must enjoy some degree of market power. Under those assumptions, every departure from marginal cost pricing reduces economic efficiency because consumers are thereby induced to purchase products which contribute less to their welfare. But those assumptions ignore the contribution that innovation makes to economic efficiency. Neither do they take account of the fact that the main commercial incentive for innovation lies in the prospect of reaping a pricing benefit from the market power which results from being first in the field with a new process or product.

Recognition of the public interest in preserving such an incentive is reflected (as noted in section F of Chapter 5) in the legal protection which is afforded to intellectual property rights – although many forms of innovation escape such protection. There is, however, no analytical basis upon which the benefits or otherwise of any particular level or duration of incentive can be estimated. In making decisions about the acceptability of the pricing policies of innovators, the competition authorities must therefore balance conflicting considerations on a judgemental basis, without the assistance of any precise public interest criterion.

Measurement Problems

Analytical and practical difficulties remain, even in connection with long-established processes and products. The use of cost-related pricing criteria leads to problems about the choice of the appropriate measure of cost. In a market in which any increase in demand would require an increase in supply capacity, the appropriate measure is *long-run marginal cost*. Where there is likely to be excess capacity, however, the choice is less clear-cut. Where the excess capacity is likely to be persistent, it will be in the public interest to set prices equal to *short-run marginal costs* in order to bring unused capacity into use. Such a practice may, however, give commercially damaging results in terms of the accounting conventions used in company accounts.

Company accounts may in any case not yield relevant measures of cost. The conventions of *historic cost accounting* lead to distortions in times of inflation, and attempts to remove such distortions by *current cost accounting* raise other problems. Capital costs may not be correctly reflected under conventional amortisation practices, and can be distorted by sale and leaseback arrangements. Current and capital costs can be distorted by the arbitrary allocation of *joint costs* among different products. Profit comparisons with other companies on the basis of *rates of return* can be misleading if the divisor used to calculate a rate is inappropriate to the activity in question.

Remedies

Further practical problems are compounded with the above difficulties when the competition authorities seek to impose the remedy of price regulation. To the problems of determining what initial price level is deemed to be in the public interest are added the problems of adjusting that level over the course of time to take account of changing commercial conditions. The availability of the information necessary for that purpose will often depend upon the unwilling cooperation of the accountants in the regulated bodies – against which the staff of the regulatory body will almost certainly be at a very considerable numerical disadvantage. The likely outcome of such a contest is hard to predict. There are dangers on the one hand of stifling risk-taking and innovation by the rigid application of arbitrary rules, and on the other hand of allowing regulation to become so permissive as to be ineffective.

In face of such difficulties, it would not be surprising if the competition authorities sought wherever possible to sidestep the issue of commercial pricing policies, and to take comfort in the prospect that competition from new entrants might eventually provide a remedy. In one case (which has already been referred to), for example, a United States court ruled that excessive pricing was pro-competitive because of the incentive it provided for new entry (*Berkey Photo 1979*).

That recourse is not, however, available in connection with natural monopolies, such as the privately-owned public utilities. There is a long and varied history of United States practice in that respect, and as British practice develops in connection with the newly-privatised public utilities, further precedents are likely to emerge. As experience grows in that connection, it may be that the criteria which emerge will be applied to other industries.

The next section of this chapter reviews the treatment by the regulatory authorities of the exploitation of market power by excessive pricing. Section C is concerned with the pricing policies of public utilities, Section D deals with price regulation, and sections E and F review the treatment by the regulatory authorities of parallel pricing and predatory pricing.

B EXCESSIVE PRICING

The Community Approach

Article 86 of the Treaty of Rome states that the charging of unfair prices by a dominant firm is an abuse of a dominant position, but gives no guidance as to what is deemed to be an unfair price. The limited amount of case law that is available indicates, however, that a price will be regarded as excessive if it appears to be high in relation to what is judged to be the *economic value* of the product.

The charging of prices for type approval certificates which were considered to be excessive in relation to the economic value of the service provided was deemed to be unfair by the European Court of Justice (*General Motors 1976, British Leyland 1987*). In both of those cases, however, the pricing policies in question had the primary purpose of restricting imports. In a case involving the supply of bananas which did not raise that issue, the Commission was unsuccessful in its attempt to establish that the prices charged were unfair. The Commission's case depended on the fact that the price charged in Denmark was more than twice that charged in Ireland, although the costs of supply were the same. The Court rejected that argument on the grounds that the Commission had not established that any profit had been made on sales in Ireland – as had first been admitted, but subsequently denied by the supplier (*United Brands 1978*).

The Court took the view in that case that adequate evidence of excessive pricing could be obtained objectively by means of an analysis of the cost structure, ascertaining the amount of the profit margin by comparison of the selling price of the product with the cost of supplying it. The question would then be whether in view of that analysis the price charged was unfair 'either in itself or when compared with competing products'. The Court acknowledged the difficulties of working out the costs of supply, but felt that in the case in question an approximate estimate should have been possible. It also acknowledged that there might be other ways of determining whether the price of a product is unfair.

The United Kingdom Approach

The treatment by the Monopolies and Mergers Commission of excessive pricing has evolved through several stages. In an early case, it found prices to be excessive by comparison with production costs obtained from the supplier (*Librium and Vallium 1978*). In subsequent cases it based its judgements upon comparisons between the *rates of return* earned by the dominant firm with those ruling in competitive markets. Eventually there was explicit recognition of the need for quantification of the concept of an *acceptable rate of return* – in relation, particularly, to the pricing policies of privately-owned public utilities. For some public utilities, that rate of return has been related to estimates of the *cost of capital* to the company in question (e.g. *Gas 1993*), and it seems possible that developments of that approach may in future be applied more widely.

The Commission has frequently emphasised, however, that the rate of return is only one of a number of factors to be taken into account in considering an appropriate level of profitability or of pricing. Some guidance as to the weight given to other factors is obtainable from a study of the cases listed in Table 3. As a broad generalisation from a study of that table, it might be concluded that prices were unlikely to have been found excessive unless rates of return were at least 50 per cent above the national average (which averaged around 17 per cent during the period covered by the table), and that rates of more than twice the average could escape condemnation in the absence of aggravating circumstances.

The Market Environment

The Commission has in fact been willing to tolerate even higher profit rates when it has perceived the market environment to be favourable to competition. In case H, although Nestlé had a 48 per cent share of the market for instant coffee, the Commission was influenced by the presence of other powerful operators in the market and the absence of significant entry barriers, and it concluded that Nestlé's unusually high profit rates must be attributable to their superior efficiency. As noted in Chapter 5, entry prospects and the possibility of competition from substitutes can be strong influences on the market environment. In case G, very high profit rates had been obtained by a monopoly supplier of tampons, but in view mainly of the prospects of competition from improved external towels and retailers' own brands, they were also attributed to superior efficiency. In case O, in the absence of such prospects, somewhat lower profit rates accruing to the same supplier had previously been taken to indicate that excessive prices were being charged. (However, in the later tampons case, the Commission were also influenced by the danger that price regulation might inhibit innovation and new entry. That problem is discussed below.)

Competition Policy in Practice

TABLE 3   *Assessments of profits in a selection of the reports of the Monopolies and Mergers Commission 1980–94*

Case[1]	Rates of return on capital for 5–6 years preceding the inquiry[2,3] annual %						(average) %	Other factors
Some cases in which prices were found not to be excessive								
A	–	14	2	17	23	24	(17)	
B	–	16	6	9	9	45	(17)	Ease of entry
C	–	15	25	22	25	16	(19)	
D	14	30	24	15	18	18	(20)	
E	24	28	13	18	37	27	(25)	
F	–	34	35	47	39	40	(39)	
G	68	58	55	68	80	68	(66)	Ease of entry
H	–	50	65	99	118	114	(89)	Competitive market
Some cases in which prices were found to be excessive								
I(a)	37	14	17	15	26	33	(24)	as supplied to MMC
(b)	64	29	29	20	30	40	(35)	as supplied to OFT
J	36	19	25	46	51	64	(40)	Complex monopoly
K	–	47	37	44	51	27	(41)	
L	46	45	53	45	35	32	(43)	Parallel pricing
M	–	54	49	47	34	32	(43)	Predatory pricing
N	61	78	69	68	91	62	(72)	Low risk product
O	102	85	94	80	67	58	(81)	Low entry prospects

Notes
[1] Case Index:

A *Contraceptive Sheaths 1994*   I *Contraceptive Sheaths 1982*
B *Animal Waste 1985*   J *Roadside Advertising 1981*
C *Liquefied Petroleum Gas 1981*   K *Animal Waste 1993*
D *Ceramic Sanitaryware 1978*   L *White Salt 1986*
E *Gas Appliances 1980*   M *Concrete Roofing Tiles 1981*
F *Ready Mixed Concrete 1981*   N *Postal Franking Machines 1986*
G *Tampons 1986*   O *Tampons 1980*
H *Soluble Coffee 1991*

[2] Historic costs basis

[3] For comparison, the average annual rate of return as obtained from a Bank of England analysis of the accounts of large companies varied between 14 and 18 per cent during the period 1978–87, and a later analysis gave average annual rates of return for manufacturing companies ranging from 13 to 21 per cent and averaging 17 per cent over the period 1989–92 (*Ice Cream 1994*).

In case *I*, a dominant market position supported by high entry barriers arising from the strength of the 'Durex' brand of condom, led the Commission to recommend price control in spite of relatively modest profit rates; but in case *A* some 12 years later, it recommended the removal of the controls in view of enhanced entry prospects and somewhat lower profit rates, although the dominant firm retained a 78 per cent market share.

Where, on the other hand, an efficient supplier earns high profits by following the price leadership of a less efficient competitor, those profits have been taken as evidence of inadequate competition. In case L, British Salt (with a 50 per cent market share) followed the price leadership of ICI (with a 45 per cent share) whose salt-producing plant was much less efficient. It was recognised that British Salt's high profits were partly due to its efficiency, but they were considered to be in part due to a lack of price competition. In the absence of entry prospects, the Commission recommended price regulation.

In the absence of any evidence of anti-competitive practices, profit rates somewhat higher than those of case I have been found not to be against the public interest. In case F, the Commission stated that it did not regard the relatively high profits of the dominant supplier (averaging 39 per cent on a historic cost basis, and 13 per cent on a current cost basis) as in themselves being evidence of abuse of monopoly power, and in the absence of any evidence of anti-competitive practices, found them not to be against the public interest. Under generally uncompetitive conditions, however, much lower profit rates have attracted criticism. In case M, the profit rates of both Redland (quoted in Table 3) and Marley (ranging from 14 to 25 per cent) were described as 'very high' in the context of their low-risk activities. Evidence of predatory pricing (as defined in section F below) to exclude new entrants was, however, a factor in that case.

Measurement Problems

Case I illustrates the great difficulty which can be experienced in estimating the rate of return on the reference product when that product gives rise to joint costs with other products in a multi-product firm. Different cost allocation methods put the rates of return reported by the supplier to the Office of Fair Trading some 50 per cent above those reported to the Monopolies and Mergers Commission. The same problem arose in case N, in which the assumptions used by the Commission were challenged by one of the suppliers. (The Commission has also faced cost allocation problems in connection with the public utilities and has, as noted in section C below, proposed some solutions in that context which may also be considered applicable to other industries.)

Rates of return on capital employed have been considered not to provide a useful measure in some service sector cases. Comparisons made on the basis of profits as a percentage of turnover were preferred in one case (case J of Table 3), and they were made on the basis of returns on equity in another (*Credit Cards 1981*).

The use of asset valuations based on historic costs can give rise to severe distortions, moreover. A return on capital employed of 47 per cent in historical cost terms reflected, in one case, the age and extent of depreciation of assets nearing the end of their useful lives. Using replacement cost valuations the average rate of return was less than 9 per cent (*Cross-Solent Ferries 1992*). Despite the almost universal use of historic cost accounts in annual reports, the use by the regulatory authorities of replacement cost adjustments in estimates of rates of return may become general.

An Acceptable Rate of Return

In considering whether prices are excessive, and in proposing regulatory remedies in monopoly cases, the Commission had, until the early 1990s, refrained from offering specific guidance as to the basis upon which it would deem the pricing policy of a monopoly to yield an acceptable rate of return. The need to regulate the pricing policies of the newly-privatised public utilities led, however, to further consideration of that question.

In relation to the pricing policies of a monopoly ferry operator, the Commission commented:

A return on capital employed on depreciated replacement cost of about 12 per cent in 1990 is somewhat above the level which has been adopted in the regulation of low-risk public utilities and, indeed, somewhat above those for the economy as a whole (the current cost accounting rate of return for all industrial and commercial companies in the UK in 1990 was 7.8 per cent – but the average over the previous 5 years was 10 per cent) ... 12 per cent is substantially toward the upper limit for a company enjoying such a strong market position – but not so high as to be regarded as excessive or to justify regulatory intervention. (*Cross-Solent Ferries 1992*)

The low-risk environment of a ferry operator placed that case in a special category, however, and in more general cases the Commission may in future make some use of risk-adjusted estimates of the company's cost of capital, by adapting the methodology used for privatised public utilities.

C PRICING POLICIES OF PUBLIC UTILITIES

The Community Dimension

The Treaty of Rome gives the European Commission powers to regulate the conduct of public ulitities where such conduct affects trade between member states (see Section H of Chapter 2). The Commission has gradually extended its exercise of those powers through the issue of regulations, recommendations and memoranda relating to specific sectors such as road, sea and air transport. A progressively widening attack is being mounted upon restrictive agreements, such as the price-fixing agreements among the major European airlines. Some of those documents also contain broad rules or guidelines concerning the general principles governing pricing policies. It has been recommended, for example, that the pricing of natural gas should be determined in the light of cost and market conditions (Council Recommendation 83/230). The practical interpretation which the Commission is likely to place upon such rules is not yet clear.

The United Kingdom Approach

In the inquiries which they have undertaken since 1991 into the pricing policies of privatised public utilities, the Monopolies and Mergers Commission have concerned themselves mainly with the implications of pricing policies for profit rates. In their efficiency audits of publicly-owned organisations in the course of the 1980s, on the other hand, the emphasis was rather on the relationship between prices and costs. The profit-related approach is considered first because of the features which it has in common with the approach which has been taken in monopoly references in recent years.

Prices and Profits

Following the criteria laid down in the various privatisation Acts, the Commission have considered that the future level of a company's prices should be such as to enable it to attract new investment and to provide its existing shareholders with a reasonable but not excessive return on their investment. The *Capital Asset Pricing Model* was found to provide an analytically coherent method of estimating a company's *cost of capital*, allowing for risks to investors; but it was found to give rise to a wide range of uncertainties arising from the variety of expert judgements which are required, and from the forecasting element in the process. Estimates of the *cost of capital* to British Gas ranged from 4 per cent to over 10 per cent (*Gas 1993*). It is clear that a good deal of further development is required before this method can produce unequivocally useful guidance.

For British Gas, the Commission concluded that a *real rate of return* of between 6.5 and 7.5 per cent on new and replacement investment would be reasonable. It did not base that conclusion only upon cost of capital considerations, but also took account of other regulatory and actual profit rates. Other regulatory rates considered were:

- for new investment by publicly owned trading organisations: 8 per cent,
- for British Airports Authority: 7 to 8 per cent.

Among actual rates considered at the time were:

- the average for 12 regional electricity companies in 1991/92: 6.8 per cent,
- the Central Statistical Office average for all industrial and commercial companies over the period 1989–91: 8.7 per cent (8.4 without North Sea)

Cost-related Pricing

In the early 1980s, the Monopolies and Mergers Commission set out the considerations which it considers should in principle govern the pricing policies of the public utilities in the following terms:

On the grounds of economic efficiency, a consumer should normally be faced, in making his decision how much to consume, with the true resource cost he imposes on the system. Conventionally, this implies some form of *marginal cost pricing*. However, long- and short-run marginal costs differ widely. Much expenditure is once-for-all capital expenditure, the costs of operating the resulting capacity being much less than that of setting it up in the first place. Once the system has been laid down, there is no straightforward argument for including more than the operating costs in marginal cost for pricing purposes – costs of past investment being regarded as 'bygones'. Indeed, if capacity is under-utilised, it is clearly reasonable to set prices at a low level (provided that operating costs are covered) in order to increase capacity utilisation. However, if demand presses on capacity, or promises to do so shortly, then the price needs to include the unit cost of prospective additions to capacity. This will ensure that the cost of additional capacity will only be incurred in response to a demonstration by consumers that they are prepared to defray the whole of it. (*Severn-Trent 1981*)

Institutional Constraints

Although considerations of economic efficiency require pricing at short-run marginal costs in situations of persistent excess capacity, the full application of such a pricing policy could impose accounting losses upon any organisation which adopted it. Such a policy is consequently ruled out by existing institutional constraints upon both publicly-owned and privately-owned public utilities.

In their investigations into publicly-owned public utilities, the Commission has acknowledged that government regulations – which stipulate required rates of return – preclude the full application of economic pricing principles. In the case of an electricity board which had an excess of generating capacity which was expected to persist for the rest of the century, it was noted that financial obligations imposed by the government precluded the general reduction in the level of tariffs which might otherwise have been expected in a situation of excess capacity (*SSEB 1986*).

It would, of course, be impracticable to impose a pricing policy which would lead to accounting losses upon a privately-owned public utility, unless some compensating subvention was also provided.

The Structure of Prices

The Commission has not, however, been prepared to accept that institutional constraints can justify the adoption of arbitrary pricing policies without regard to their effect upon economic efficiency. In the electricity board case which has been referred to, the Commission proposed a change in the relation between the 'standing charge' (which was applied to the first block of units of electricity consumed) and the additional charge which was made for each additional unit consumed. Its proposal was designed to bring surplus capacity into use by reducing the additional charge, while offsetting any consequent revenue loss by an increase in the standing charge.

Similar adjustments have been recommended in order to improve the utilisation of the surplus capacity which exists during 'off-peak' periods in the supply of services by some public utilities. In an investigation of rail fares, the Commission was critical of the fact that off-peak fares were very little lower than peak fares, despite the fact that the incremental cost of off-peak travel was relatively small (*British Rail 1987*). It was estimated that a reduction in off-peak fares could result in a loss of revenue in some segments of the rail network, but that demand was sufficiently price-sensitive in other segments for fare reductions to maintain or improve revenue. In another inquiry it was noted that it was cheaper to supply gas on an 'interruptable basis' than on a 'firm basis' because the former arrangement relieved the supplier of the need to instal extra storage capacity by enabling it to interrupt supplies during periods of peak demand. The supplier's policy of restricting such interruptable supplies was found to be against the public interest (*Gas 1988*).

Information Requirements

The implementation of the principles which the Commission has put forward for the structuring of prices may require the collection of data which is not available from existing information systems. In the rail fares case, for example, it was recommended that the market responsiveness to off-peak fare reductions should be tested. Implementation of the Commission's recommendations would also require changes to the cost accounting system which, it was noted, was largely directed to budgetary control rather than the identification of the costs of particular operations.

Existing methods of allocating *joint costs* between different activities may also have to be changed. The Commission has, for example, criticised the methods used for the allocation of the costs of gas showrooms as between the selling of appliances, the settling of bills and other services, as a result of which it was impossible to tell whether the retailing operations were cost-effective (*Gas Appliances 1980*). The Commission itself recommended the allocation of showroom costs according to time spent and space used in one case (*SWEB 1984*). In another case, a more fundamental method was proposed to determine whether appliance retailing was an economic operation, or whether it was being subsidised out of electricity prices. The Commission rejected the Board's contention that all its showrooms would be retained if appliance sales were withdrawn, and recommended that a review should be undertaken of alternative ways of providing non-retailing services if showrooms were closed, in order to find out what costs should be allocated to those services (*SSEB 1986*).

It has been accepted, however, that the costs of obtaining the information needed for a cost-related pricing system may outweigh its benefits. The costs of a metering system for water supply were, for example, estimated narrowly to outweigh the benefits from such a system (*Severn-Trent Water 1981*). It was recommended that charges based arbitrarily upon rateable value should be continued, for the want of a better alternative.

D   PRICE REGULATION

In view of its practical difficulties and of its economic drawbacks, the Commission has been reluctant to recommend price regulation where it could see any reasonable alternative. Its attitude has been explained in the following terms:

> Regulation of prices ... may be justified where the prospects of promoting a more competitive environment are remote; on the other hand it may discourage the investment, innovation and new entry that would otherwise be expected to reduce prices and to improve the range of goods available to the public. (*Tampons 1986*)

Concern about the drawbacks of price regulation has in two cases influenced the Commission toward finding pricing not to be against the public interest (*Petrol 1979, Tampons 1986*), but in another case excessive pricing was found to be against the public interest although no remedy was proposed (*Tampons 1980*). Wherever possible, the Commission have preferred to recommend action designed to encourage new entrants into the market or otherwise to strengthen competition. In making recommendations, the Commission have in any case to look to the future, and account has been taken of the prospect of price reductions following new entry (*Plasterboard 1990*).

There has been a tendency in reports on monopoly references to frame such regulatory regimes as have been recommended in simple and limited terms, such as 'no price increases for three years, followed by a pricing review' (e.g. *White Salt 1986*). The need to recommend specific measures of price regulation cannot, however, be avoided when pricing by a public utility is referred to the Commission under the provisions of privatisation legislation. In such cases more complex restrictions have been imposed. Formulae have been used which relate permitted price movements to movements in the Retail Prices Index (referred to as 'RPI minus X'). The permitted price increases have in some cases been related to the weighted average price of a 'basket' of tariffs (as in the case of British Telecom) and in other cases have been expressed in terms of total revenue yield per unit of output. The Commission has noted that the 'basket' formula provided an incentive to concentrate price increases on those elements of the basket for which demand was growing fastest. The revenue yield approach, on the other hand, was considered to present the greater danger that otherwise unprofitable business would be sought by reducing output-related charges and more than compensating for the resulting losses by increasing other charges (*Manchester Airport 1987*).

E   PARALLEL PRICING AND INFORMATION AGREEMENTS

In most spheres of business, explicit agreements to regulate suppliers' prices are effectively prohibited by both Article 85(1) of the Treaty of Rome and the Restrictive Trade Practices Act 1976 (exceptions are noted in section B of Chapter 2). The legislation has also been used to prohibit the exchange of pricing information and other commercially sensitive information. The prohibitions are not confined to written agreements or exchanges: under both EU and British law, an agreement can be inferred from informal communications:

> all that is required is that the parties should have communicated with one another in some way, and that as a result of that communication, each has intentionally aroused in the other an expectation that he will act in a certain way. (Cross J in *Basic Slag 1957*) (For a similar judgement under EU law see *Suiker Unie 1976*.)

European Union Practice

Participation in meetings with competitors for the purpose of influencing their conduct has been considered to be a concerted practice (*Polypropylene 1991, Netherlands Construction 1992*) In a market dominated by four firms, a system of confidential information exchange has been condemned even in the absence of other evidence of anti-competitive pricing practices, on the grounds that it restricted the hidden competition which would otherwise exist and formed a barrier to new market entrants, (*UK Tractor 1992*). Moreover a concerted practice can be deemed to exist even if there is no communication between the parties concerned:

> it is sufficient for an independent undertaking knowingly and of its own accord to adjust its behaviour in line with the wishes of another undertaking. (*Hasselblad 1982*)

The occurrence of parallel price movements is not regarded on its own as evidence of a concerted practice, but – as noted by the European Court of Justice in a case involving the parallel pricing of dyestuffs – it may be strong evidence of such a practice:

> when it leads to conditions of competition which do not correspond to the normal conditions of the market . . . Such is the case especially where the parallel behaviour is such as to permit the parties to seek price equilibrium at a different level from that which would have resulted from competition. (*ICI 1972*)

In that case it was concluded that the parallel price movements of a wide range of products which were observed in different national markets in the Community could not be explained by market conditions because each market was dominated by a local supplier. The purpose of the practice was seen to be the preservation of that pattern of dominance by avoiding price competition. Where market conditions offer a plausible alternative explanation for parallel price movements, however, that explanation has been accepted (as in the case of some of the local markets for sugar in the case of *Suiker Unie 1976*, 4th infringement.) A deliberate *transparency of prices* among a large number of suppliers, together with evidence of parallel price movements was condemned by the Commission (*Woodpulp 1985*). The decision however, was overruled by the European Court of Justice after independent experts had found that such movements could alternatively be explained by market forces. The court ruled that:

> parallel conduct cannot be regarded as furnishing proof of concertation unless concertation constitutes the only plausible explanation of such conduct. (*Woodpulp 1993*)

(For an analysis of the Woodpulp case and its consequences, see van Gerven and Varin 1994.)

United Kingdom Practice

Agreements to regulate prices must be registered under the Restrictive Trade Practices Act and are certain to be prohibited by the Court. A company is held to be responsible for the actions of its employees in that respect, even if it had specifically prohibited those actions (*Smiths' Concrete 1991* as confirmed by the House of Lords in 1994). However, parallel pricing which does not result from some communication between the parties is not registrable under the Restrictive Trade Practices Act. It may, however, constitute evidence of the existence of a 'complex monopoly' (as defined in section E of Chapter 2) under the Fair Trading Act, and thus bring within the scope of a monopoly reference firms which would otherwise not quality for investigation. In its inquiries into those and other monopoly references, the Monopolies and Mergers Commission has in a number of cases found the practice of parallel pricing to be against the public interest.

The Commission has defined parallel pricing as:

the practice of two or more suppliers . . . when effecting changes in prices . . . of doing so at or about the same time and by the same or a similar amount or proportion. (*Parallel Pricing 1973*)

Parallel pricing is not on its own normally considered to be against the public interest, however, unless it is accompanied by evidence of excessive profits (*Flour and Bread 1977*). The publication by the British Medical Association of guidelines for consultants' fees was, however, declared to be against the public interest because those fees were consequently higher than they would otherwise be (*Medical Services 1994*).

Similarities in the movements of suppliers' price lists have not necessarily been taken to amount to parallel pricing. (*Petrol 1990*) Competitive discounting from such lists has in several cases been taken to indicate the existence of price competition (*Ceramic Sanitaryware 1978, Insulated Wires and Cables 1979, Steel Wire Fencing 1987*). In one case, however, the granting of special discounts to large customers was not considered to reflect adequate price competition because they were too localised and their effect on average prices was too small (*Concrete Roofing Tiles 1981*).

Like the European Commission, the Monopolies and Mergers

Commission has acknowledged that in some cases competitive market conditions may plausibly provide an alternative explanation of similar and simultaneous price movements. In cases in which suppliers' costs were similar, the Commission has often been inclined to accept that explanation. Similarities in profit rates – together with evidence of ease of entry – were additional factors taken to support the Commission's conclusions in two of the above cases (*Ceramic Sanitaryware 1978, Insulated Wires and Cables 1979*).

An explicit acknowledgement that it was prepared in principle, and under some circumstances, to accept a competitive explanation appeared in one report in the following terms:

> In current conditions in this industry – particularly the complete interchangeability of the products, well-informed buyers, and manufacturers with spare capacity and costs sensitive to volume – we accept that the force of competition is bound to lead to a similarity of published prices. No one manufacturer could, for more than a short period, sustain a higher published price without losing significant volume to any of its competitors who had the capacity to produce more, or a lower published price without his competitors matching him to avoid a loss of volume. Significant differences would be expected to occur only when the price leader was attempting to initiate a change which others were refusing to follow, or from which others were seeking to secure some competitive advantage by delaying their reaction. (*Electricity Supply Meters 1979*, par 135)

Despite that acknowledgement, the Commission concluded in the case in question that the pricing policies of the two leading suppliers amounted to the creation of a complex monopoly situation and that the situation operated against the public interest because its effect was to raise prices and to reduce competitive pressures.

The main consideration which led the Commission to reject a competitive explanation in the above case was the persistence of a similarity of prices in the face of wide differences in costs. In the case of *White Salt* 1986, which has been referred to in the previous section of this chapter, that consideration was reinforced by a long history of arrangements designed to restrict price competition. In an earlier case, however, a close similarity of prices and price movements over a five-year period was not interpreted as evidence of uncompetitive behaviour despite substantial cost differences. The return on capital employed of the dominant supplier of pet foods (with a 50 per cent market share) had averaged 44 per cent, as compared with the 19 per cent earned by its closest rival (with a 30 per cent share). Prices had, however, fallen in real terms, and competition from new entrants and from the use of household scraps was expected to limit the suppliers' ability to raise prices in the future (*Cat and Dog Foods 1977*).

F   PREDATORY PRICING

Since, by definition, the purpose of predatory pricing is to exclude competition by selective undercutting, any policy which can be identified as having that purpose or effect is bound to be condemned by the regulatory authorities. Certainty of condemnation when the practice is identified is not, however, matched by certainty of identification. In the absence of evidence of intent, it is often by no means easy to distinguish between anti-competitive predatory pricing on the one hand, and the acceptable tactics of normal price competition on the other. American lawyers have proposed that the criterion for drawing that distinction should be:

(a) that only if prices are set below *short-run marginal costs* should they be considered to be predatory; but that,
(b) in view of the difficulty of measuring marginal costs, *average variable cost* is a generally acceptable surrogate. (Areeda and Turner, 1975)

The Areeda-Turner rules are, however, open to the criticism that they are too lenient because a firm which sets its prices at a level which does not enable the cost of capital investment to be recovered, and which does not cover joint or overhead costs, might thereby force others out of business.

European Union Practice

Predatory pricing normally implies price discrimination, which is prohibited by Article 86 where it involves a dominant firm:

applying dissimilar conditions to equivalent transactions with other trading parties, thereby placing them at a competitive disadvantage.

Moreover, it has been shown that the practice of charging different prices in different national markets cannot be defended on the grounds that those prices were set in line with the different conditions of demand or competition in those markets. Price discrimination on those grounds has been condemned (*United Brands 1978*). Fidelity rebates not related to costs have similarly been considered abusive (*Hoffman-La Roche 1975*).

In the only case which was specifically concerned with predatory pricing, however, the Commission relied upon evidence of intent contained in company documents which it had obtained using its powers under Regulation 17 (see section B of Chapter 3) (*ECS/AKZO 1986*). In that case the Commission rejected a defence under the Areeda-Turner rule that the allegedly abusive prices had always been above average variable costs, basing its findings on evidence of AKZO's predatory intent. In upholding the Commission's findings, the European Court of Justice ruled that, while pricing below average variable cost is necessarily predatory and therefore abusive, pricing above average variable cost but below total cost will be regarded as abusive when it is part of a campaign aimed at destroying a rival (*AKZO v Commission 1991*).

United Kingdom Practice

The Office of Fair Trading has stated that in assessing whether a firm's behaviour is vigorous competition or predation it focuses on three types of evidence:

> whether the structure and characteristics of the market and the alleged predator are such as to make predation a sensible and feasible business strategy; whether the alleged predator incurs losses arising from the course of conduct; and, what the intentions of the alleged predator are – taking into account any relevant evidence of its behaviour in other markets. (*Thamesway 1993*)

In some cases the practice has been abandoned before a formal investigation under the Competition Act had been started. For example, the Scottish Milk Marketing Board agreed in 1982 to abandon a pricing practice which discriminated against its competitors, and to align its pricing structure more closely to its costs; and in 1985, Grey-Green Coaches withdrew a free travel offer which might have had the effect of eliminating new competition.

In some of its early reports the Commission condemned covert price-cutting devices which were designed specifically to exclude competition, such as secretly-owned brands (*Matches 1953*) and 'fighting companies' (*Industrial Gases 1956*). In later years it made adverse public interest findings in cases of extreme price differentiation which was clearly designed to keep competitors out of particular parts of a market (*Librium & Vallium 1973, Contraceptive Sheaths 1975, Gas 1988*).

All of those cases were clear-cut because of either the intent or the extent of the selective price-cutting. It was not until 1981 that a case arose which required a detailed analysis of the relationship between costs and prices. It was alleged in that case that the suppliers of, respectively, 46 per cent and 36 per cent of the UK market for concrete roofing tiles had used selective discounting to counter competition from a new entrant in Scotland. The test which, in the view of the leading supplier, should be used to reconcile the legitimate interests of the new entrant with those of the established companies was that prices which were above average variable cost should be presumed to be competitive rather than predatory unless:

(a) there was no objective justification for the pricing policy;
(b) the policy was substantially exclusionary in purpose or effect; and,
(c) the elimination of the competition may reasonably be expected to result in a detriment to the public interest.

The leading supplier demonstrated to the Commission's satisfaction that its lowest prices were well in excess of its average variable costs. The Commission also accepted that there was an objective commercial justification for the pricing policy and that it fell short of a deliberate intention to eliminate the competitor at all costs. It nevertheless concluded that the policy acted as a barrier to entry and that in the circumstances of that industry it would be expected to operate against the public interest. In effect, the Commission thus rejected the proposed test without offering any alternative.

The Office of Fair Trading has since taken the view that prices may be predatory where they exceed short-run marginal costs, but are less than average total cost. It has stated, however, that it does not consider that a pricing policy which leads to accounting losses, because capital and overhead costs are not covered, can unambiguously be said to be predatory. It considers that in such cases evidence of intent and of the nature of the market must be taken into account. The pricing policies of a supplier of hypodermic syringes were found not to be anti-competitive because they were above average total cost (but excluding any return on capital employed), because there was no evidence of predatory intent and because the dominance of the National Health Service as a buyer in the market, and the absence of other entry barriers, made it unlikely that a predatory pricing strategy could be successful (*Becton Dickinson 1988*).

The pricing policy of a supplier of condoms to the National Health Service was nevertheless found to be predatory although variable costs and some fixed costs were covered, because the aim was to damage a competitor (*Contraceptive Sheaths 1994*). In the absence of clear evidence that the supplier was seeking to drive a competitor from the market, pricing which led to significant losses was not found to be predatory (*Animal Waste 1993*)

Since the privatisation of UK bus services, the Office of Fair Trading has had many complaints about predation, including aggressive scheduling ('leapfrogging') as well as predatory prices. Underpricing usually occurred on selected routes, and in a clear-cut case where the prices charged did not even cover the drivers' wages, price control was recommended (*Southdown 1993*). In another case, action was taken against leapfrogging but control of what was found to be predatory pricing was considered impracticable, even though the prices charged for some additional journeys did not cover variable cost (*Kent Buses 1993*).

ANNEX 7.1 TERMINOLOGY

Average variable cost
The average cost per unit of output, excluding those costs which remain constant in the short- to medium-term (used as a surrogate for short-run marginal cost in the Areeda-Turner criteria for predatory pricing).

Beta
The ratio of the variability of the price of a security to the variability of the total price of market as a whole (used in the Capital Asset Pricing Model).

Capital Asset Pricing Model (CAPM)
The theory that the rate of return which an equity investor expects from a particular security is given by the available riskless rate, plus the security's Beta, times the equity market's risk premium (that risk

premium being the excess of the market's average return over the riskless rate). See Blake (1990) p. 297.

Cost of capital
The weighted average cost of equity and debt to a company (for sample calculations see *Gas 1993* appendix 7.3).

Current cost accounting (CCA)
Accounting systems in which all costs and values are adjusted to current price levels.

Economic value
A term used (but not defined) by the European Court of Justice in connection with excessive pricing. The cost of production and pricing by competitors were both considered relevant (*United Brands 1978*).

Historic cost accounting (HCA)
The conventional accounting system under which the costs and valuations used are those ruling at the time of manufacture or purchase.

Joint costs
Costs which are attributable to more than one class of output.

Long-run marginal cost (LRMC)
The cost of increasing output by one unit over a sustained period including the cost of increasing output capacity.

Marginal cost
The cost of producing one additional unit of output.

Operating profit
Profit before deducting tax, interest, extraordinary items or dividends.

Real rate of return
The rate of return corrected for inflation.

Required rate of return (RRR)
The rate of return required by HM Treasury to be earned on new investment by publicly-owned bodies (set in 1989 at 8 per cent for trading organisations and 6 per cent for non-trading organisations). See HM Treasury (1991).

Return on capital employed (ROCE)
Operating profit as a percentage of total of shareholder's capital and
retained profit, revaluation reserves, borrowings less cash balances and
minority interests.

Return on net assets (RONA)
Operating profit as a percentage net assets, as shown on the company's
balance sheet.

Return on turnover (*ROT*)
Operating profit as a percentage of total sales.

Rate of return (ROR)
A term used by the MMC to denote operating profit as a percentage
of capital employed or of net assets or of turnover (see separate definitions).

Short-run marginal cost (SRMC)
The cost of increasing output by one unit when this does not require
an increase in output capacity.

8 Distribution

A INTRODUCTION

As the previous chapter has shown, the competition authorities are in
principle prepared to regulate transactions between suppliers and consumers when the market power of suppliers puts consumer at a disadvantage. The functions of intermediaries between supplier and consumer
raise further issues when those functions go beyond that of competing
freely in the provision of services to consumers. Competition issues
arise, for example, when the intermediaries themselves acquire market
power, or when they are used to enhance the market power of suppliers.
Under effects-based policies, however, the consequences for competition have to be balanced against any associated gains in efficiency and
quality of service.

The Market Power of Distributors

The regulatory authorities in Britain and elsewhere in the Community
have exhibited some concern about the growth of concentration in some
retailing areas, particularly in food retailing by supermarkets.

In Britain, three large firms now account for over 50 per cent of
supermarket grocery sales. The Monopolies and Mergers Commission
has drawn attention to fears that a handful of large multiples might
come to dominate the distributive trades, to the disadvantage of suppliers and consumers (*Discounts to Retailers 1981*), and the Government has indicated that any proposed acquisitions by those large multiples
should be referred to the Commission (*Hansard*, 27 January 1988).
However, the mergers which have occurred have usually involved only
the smaller supermarket chains, and have escaped reference on the ground
that they would serve to strengthen their ability to compete with the
large chains. No evidence of abuse of distributors' market power has
yet emerged, the indications being that they use that power mainly to
buy produce at reduced prices, and that most of the savings are passed
on to consumers.

Joint Buying

In France and in West Germany, there has been concern that the practice among small retailers of forming 'buying groups' in order to obtain discounts from their suppliers, has recently spread to the larger
retailing chains, with the formation of 'super buying groups'. However, inquiries by the regulatory authorities have generally led to the
conclusion that the market power of the larger groups has not yet reached
such a level as to warrant intervention.

Concern by the European Commission has led to the commissioning
of a special study of the effects of concentration in retailing, but the
authors concluded that the buying power of distributors had not generally been abused (Comp report 16, 1987, p. 236). The European Court
has ruled that joint buying associations which impose no exclusive
buying obligations on their members will not normally be held to infringe Article 85(1) of the Treaty (*Spar 1975*), and the Commission
has indicated that it would in any case be willing to grant exemptions
where the agreement enables retailers to obtain fair terms and does
not put undue pressure on suppliers. The Commission has given approval to an *European Economic Interest Grouping* (EEIG) of seven
medium-sized pharmaceutical wholesalers, which incorporated a buying agreement under which members remained free to determine prices
and conditions of sale of their products (*EEIG Orphe 1990*).

In the United Kingdom, the Office of Fair Trading has issued the
following guidance concerning the circumstances under which it would
seek an order (as described in section C of Chapter 3) not to proceed
against a joint buying agreement in the Restrictive Practices Court:

A number of agreements for group buying include recommendations for the price to be charged for goods covered by special promotions of 'own brand' goods. Such recommendations are likely to
be registrable restrictions but may not be considered significantly
anti-competitive if members are free to charge lower prices if they
wish and, in the case of promotions, provided that those are for a
short time and the recommended price is lower than that usually
charged.

Some sorts of restrictions in group buying agreements have had
to be modified or abandoned before representations could be made.
These include:
– allocation of geographical areas to particular members
– wholesalers not to supply or sponsor retailers outside defined areas

- wholesalers or retailers to purchase minimum quantities through the group
- members not to join any other group.
   (OFT guides: Restrictive Practices.)

The Influence of Suppliers upon Distributors

The remainder of this chapter is concerned with the treatment by the regulatory authorities of practices adopted by suppliers in their dealings with distributors. Generally speaking, that treatment depends upon the nature of the commercial relationship between supplier and distributor, and upon the effect of the practice upon third parties.

The authorities rarely intervene when the commercial relationship is that of common ownership, except when the practice excludes third parties from a major part of a market. They are also reluctant to prohibit any practice which is a necessary part of a freely negotiated commercial agreement such as an agency or a franchise. Section B below reviews the treatment of practices arising under such arrangements.

Intervention is frequently considered, however, when a supplier imposes restrictions upon independent distributors. Sections C, D, and E review the treatment under those circumstances of exclusive and selective distribution, exclusive dealing and full-line forcing.

B   RESTRICTIONS AS PART OF A COMMERCIAL RELATIONSHIP

Selective distribution, exclusive dealing and full-line forcing (which – as noted in sections C–E below – may be considered to be anti-competitive practices when they are imposed upon an independent retailer) are often part and parcel of the everyday dealings between the supplying and retailing divisions of a single company. As such, they may escape regulation when they are seen as concomitants of the normal commercial advantages of that type of business organisation. They may escape regulation for the same reason when they are a customary part of certain other commercial relationships. The authorities are nonetheless not prepared to exonerate restrictive practices under those circumstances unless they are necessary to secure the efficiency advantages which accrue to those forms of organisation.

Franchising

Franchise agreements commonly restrict the franchisee's sources of supply
and the geographical area in which he may operate. In return, the
franchisor may undertake to limit the number of competing outlets to
which franchises are granted.

The European Commission has published a block exemption for franchise agreements containing a wide range of specified restrictions, subject
to a few conditions, including:

(a) the exclusion of reciprocal franchising agreements between com-
    peting suppliers;
(b) the requirement that the franchisee should be free to set resale
    prices;
(c) the requirement that the franchisee should be free to obtain sup-
    plies of the product from other franchisees or authorised dealers.
(d) the requirement that the franchisee must reveal its status as an
    independent undertaking.
    (Regulation 4087/88 of 30 November 1988)

The Director-General of Fair Trading has advised that franchise agreements are likely to be registrable under the Restrictive Trade Practices
Act if both franchisor and franchisee accept restrictions, but that geo-
graphic restrictions are generally unobjectionable except when:

(a) they are more than is reasonably necessary for the operation of
    the franchise; or,
(b) the agreement disguises a market sharing arrangement.

The Director of the Office of Fair Trading's Competition Division has
reported that most registrable franchising agreements have been regarded as acceptable to the extent that the procedure of Section 21(2)
of the Act has been used to avoid proceeding against them (see section C of Chapter 3). A restriction upon the franchisor not to compete
in the territory of the franchisee is not likely to be an obstacle to that
procedure if there is keen inter-brand competition, nor is there likely
to be any objection to a restriction upon the franchisee not to supply
goods outside his territory. Recommended prices are not considered
objectionable provided that the franchisee is free to charge lower prices
(Howe, 1988).

The Monopolies and Mergers Commission has indicated that no public interest issue is likely to arise from an obligation on a franchisee to obtain goods only from his franchisor, provided that:

(a) the goods could be regarded as an essential part of the franchise packet;
(b) their precise nature and quality standards are important; and,
(c) the goods could not readily and without disadvantage be obtained elsewhere.
(*Full Line Forcing 1981*)

Exclusive buying conditions have, for example, been considered to be justified in the case of mobile vans and ice cream parlours, franchised for the sale of branded ice cream, which were prominently identified by a supplier who provided support in terms of finance or of advice and training (*Ice Cream 1979*). On the other hand, the requirement that franchised car dealers should buy replacement parts only from the car manufacturer was considered to be against the public interest because the dealers could otherwise have obtained similar parts from independent component manufacturers (*Car Parts 1982*). However, the refusal of car manufacturers to supply parts except to their franchised dealers was later found not to be against the public interest, although it was considered to be a matter of 'potential concern' (*Car Parts 1992*).

Agency

Commercial agents, who negotiate or conclude transactions on behalf of principals, may under some circumstances escape regulation.

The European Commission has advised that exclusive agencies of that type fall outside the prohibition of Article 85(1) of the Treaty and need not be notified, provided that the agent does not bear any of the risks of the transactions. Article 85(1) is, however, likely to apply if the agent:

(a) maintains substantial stocks at his own expense;
(b) provides a substantial free service to customers at his own expense; or,
(c) is free to determine prices or terms of business.
(Commission Notice of 24 December 1962, JO 1962 2921)

Article 85(1) has been held also to apply if the agent trades on his own account in the same commodity (*Suiker Unie 1976*), and may apply if he acts for competing suppliers (Article 3 of Regulation 1983/83, referred to in section C below) – even if he bears none of the risks arising from agency transactions. Article 85(1) does not apply to the appointment of an agent for a product in a given territory unless there is some restriction upon the action of the agent or his principal, or competition is otherwise affected. The Commission decided that the International Air Transport Association's (IATA) system of accredited marketing agents was subject to Article 85(1), even after unnecessary restrictions had been removed because little room remained for any other means of marketing air travel and freight. Exemption was granted under Article 85(3), however, after restrictions preventing IATA agents from working for non-IATA airlines (and vice-versa) had been removed.

Agency agreements normally escape regulation under the present Restrictive Trade Practices Act because that act does not apply to agreements between suppliers of goods and suppliers of services or because Section 9(3) of the act excludes terms in an agreement which relate exclusively to the goods supplied.

The Monopolies and Mergers Commission has noted that although the appointment of agencies restricts competition, the consumer benefits from better choice in the manufacturer's range and from better technical advice. The public interest is not in its view likely to be affected unless competition is unduly restricted (*Full Line Forcing 1981*). The practice by a supplier of automotive components of forbidding its service agents - but not its other distributors – from buying competing components from other suppliers was considered not to be against the public interest because those agents were considered to be part of the supplier's distribution organisation (*Car Parts 1982*). The Commission did not fundamentally object to the selective and exclusive distribution system imposed by car manufacturers on dealers acting as factors, but sought the removal of some inessential restrictions (*Cars 1992*).

Restrictions Arising from Common Ownership

In the European Community, the acquisition by a dominant supplier of a sufficient proportion of wholesale or retail outlets to enable it to restrict competition could be prohibited under Article 86 as an abuse of a dominant position, but there is no recorded case of such a prohibition.

In the United Kingdom, the Monopolies and Mergers Commission has drawn attention to dangers to the public interest if company-owned outlets were to provide a very high proportion of retail sales in any major retail market (*Petrol 1979*, par 148). In that case it did not, however, regard company ownership of 30 per cent of retail outlets for petrol, accounting for 50 per cent of retail sales, as being against the public interest – thereby reversing an earlier decision (*Petrol 1965*).

The ownership by brewers of 86 per cent of the public houses in England and Wales and their operation of the 'tied house system' were, however, found to operate against the public interest because they created entry barriers and detriments to efficiency and to the interests of consumers (*Beer 1969*). The appropriate remedy was at that time considered to be reform of the licensing system. Following a subsequent inquiry, it was recommended on similar grounds that no brewer should be allowed to own or lease or have an interest in more than 2000 on-licensed outlets (*Beer 1989*). (A total ban on the ownership of licensed premises by brewers was rejected in order to protect those local brewers who are entirely dependent upon their tied estates because they do not have the resources to promote their brands nationally.) That recommendation was eventually rejected by Lord Young, the then Secretary of State, but the major brewers were ordered to relax some of the restrictions imposed upon their tenants in respect of half of the pubs owned by each brewer in excess of 2000.

C   EXCLUSIVE AND SELECTIVE DISTRIBUTION

Restrictions upon competition may also be deemed to occur when a supplier restricts his sales in a particular area to a single distribution outlet (*exclusive distribution*) and when a supplier seeks to limit the type or number of distribution outlets through which his product may be sold (*selective distribution*).

Both practices imply the *refusal to supply* to other outlets, and they are frequently associated with other restrictions upon competition. The further restrictions which arise when a supplier requires a distributor not to make purchases from competing suppliers are also considered in section D, *Exclusive Dealing*.

Exclusive Distribution

The regulatory authorities in the European Community have consistently condemned collective exclusive distribution agreements. Bilateral exclusive distribution agreements, on the other hand, have been held generally to lead to an improvement in distribution. Their use as a means of imposing resale price maintenance or of restricting exports or parallel imports has been prohibited (*Junghans 1977, Zanussi 1978*).

Bilateral exclusive distribution agreements concerning goods are otherwise exempt from Article 85(1) of the Treaty of Rome, subject to a number of conditions. To gain exemption they must place no restriction upon the supplier other than an obligation not to supply the contract goods to others in the contract territory, and they must place no obligations upon the distributor except:

(a) not to manufacture or distribute goods which compete with the contract goods;
(b) to obtain goods for resale only from the supplier;
(c) to refrain from seeking customers or establishing branches or depots outside the contract territory (but there must not be a ban on selling outside the contract territory);
(d) to purchase complete ranges or minimum quantities;
(e) to sell the contract goods under trademarks or packed and presented as specified by the supplier; or,
(f) to advertise promote and provide customer services for the product;

– nor must there be obstacles which make it difficult for purchasers to obtain the goods from outside the contract territory.

The exemption does not apply where there are reciprocal exclusive dealing agreements between competing manufacturers nor where there is a non-reciprocal agreement involving a manufacturer with a turnover of more than 100 million ECU. It may be withdrawn by the Commission in particular cases. (See Regulation 1983/83, OJ 1983 L173/1 & L281/24 and also the Commission Notice OJ 1984 C101/2.)

In the United Kingdom, collective exclusive distribution agreements are registrable under the Restrictive Trade Practices Act 1976 and are effectively prohibited. Bilateral agreements are not registrable but unilateral and bilateral exclusive distribution can at present be investigated under the Competition Act. As a result of such investigations the British Railways Board and the British Airports Authority have, for example, abandoned the practice of restricting those who may provide taxi or self-drive car hire services at their stations and airports. The Director-General has indicated, however, that exclusive concessions of that type would not necessarily be considered to be anti-competitive if there were competition in the relevant market or if the concessions were awarded by competitive tendering at regular intervals (*British Airports Authority: Gatwick Airport 1984*).

Selective Distribution: Qualitative Criteria

Refusal to supply other than to retailers who meet criteria laid down by manufacturers has sometimes been approved by the competition authorities, even where price competition is thereby restricted. The European Court have confined approval to:

> high-quality and high-technology products which may justify a reduction of price competition in favour of competition relating to factors other than price. (*AEG Telefunken 1983*)

Approval has frequently been made conditional upon the removal of restrictions which the authorities have considered to be unnecessary. In the particular case of motor vehicles, there is automatic exemption from Article 85(1) for arrangements complying with Regulation 123/85 which permits a range of restrictions including restrictions upon sales of competitors' products. For other qualifying products, however, exemption of selective distribution agreements has not been given unless:

(a) they are based only upon objective criteria such as financial stability and the adequacy of staff and facilities;
(b) those criteria are reasonably necessary to ensure an adequate distribution of the goods in question;
(c) supply is not refused to anyone who meets those criteria nor permitted to anyone who does not; and,
(d) the distributor is free to set his own prices and to deal in competing products.

The European Court has indicated, however, that should such a selective distribution system become so general as effectively to exclude other forms of distribution, the exemption would cease to apply (*Metro 1987*).

Other products requiring technically qualified retailers for which exemptions have been granted have included cameras (*Kodak 1970*) electronic equipment (*Metro 1987, Grundig 1994*) and personal computers (*IBM 1984*) but a requirement that cosmetic products could be sold only by qualified practising pharmacists was considered to go beyond what was necessary to maintain the quality and proper use of the product (*Vichy 1991*). Restrictions designed solely to preserve brand images have also been exempted in cases involving up-market perfumes (*Yves Saint Laurent 1992 and Givenchy 1992*) and crystal glass (*Baccarat 1991*).

In Britain, refusal to supply to a distributor because he is a price-cutter is unlawful under Section 11 of the Resale Prices Act 1976. But prohibition can be avoided by claiming that there are other reasons for refusal, and by other methods (see DTI 1979 pp. 51–3). Refusal to supply may, however, be investigated under the Competition Act 1980, which was introduced partly for that purpose. Other types of exclusive supply may be investigated under Section 17 of the Competition Act. The first such investigation concerned the selective use of qualitative criteria by a dominant bicycle manufacturer in order to avoid supplying discount stores. The criteria included the provision of pre-delivery inspection and assembly, but that requirement was not applied consistently, as evidenced by the fact that 19 per cent of the manufacturer's bicycles were supplied to mail-order firms who did not offer those facilities. Although the Monopolies and Mergers Commission concluded that the practice was against the public interest, it effectively sanctioned its continuation by recommending only that the manufacturer should be required not to refuse supply to retailers who provide adequate pre-delivery inspection and assembly (*Bicycles 1981*). Refusal to supply power tools to discounters was subsequently found to be against the public interest (*Black and Decker 1989*) but refusal to supply perfumes to the *Superdrug* retailer was approved on the grounds similar to those employed by the European Commission, namely that:

> fine fragrances are marketed as luxury products and suppliers need to be able to control their distribution in order to protect the brand images which consumers evidently value. (*Fine Fragrances 1993*)

A prohibition by a supplier of the renting of its video games was found to be against the public interest because it

> deprives consumers of an important opportunity to experience games and make informed purchases. (*Video Games 1995*)

Selective Distribution: Quantitative Criteria

A somewhat different treatment is accorded to restrictions by suppliers upon the number of distributive outlets in a particular area. In an early case, the European Commission exempted such an agreement concerning watches (*Omega 1970*) but subsequently the Commission stated that in such cases exemptions under Article 85(3) can be granted only in exceptional circumstances, and then only when the technical or other nature of the product is such that there must be close cooperation between manufacturer and dealer which could not be secured under some other system (Comp Report 5, 1976). The block exemption for motor vehicles permits such restrictions, but exemptions for other products have been rare.

In Britain, the practice has been considered to be justified under a range of circumstances. The Monopolies and Mergers Commission has noted that among the supplier's motives might be:

(a) that to add to the number of outlets would increase his distribution costs without increasing his sales; or,
(b) that he would do better by catering for a limited class of customer who is prepared to pay for exclusiveness.

The Commission saw no reason to treat refusal to supply for either of those reasons as being against the public interest when it is practised under reasonably competitive conditions (*Refusal to Supply 1970*). In cases involving very limited competition among suppliers, the practice has been considered in several cases to be justified by its effects on distributors. It was considered to be in the public interest for the dominant wholesalers of newspapers to limit the number of retailers which they supplied and to select them on the basis of their location (*Newpapers 1978 and 1993*), and a similar practice was accepted in the bicycles case discussed above. Competition considerations were in those cases taken to be outweighed by the public interest in maintaining an effective distribution system, although the reports contained little by way of analysis of the consequences of relaxing the restrictions. The general argument that without restrictions on their numbers, retailers would lose profits and press for increased margins was accepted in one case (*Infant Milk Foods 1967*) but rejected in another (*Colour Film 1966*). In the latter case the Commission thought that Kodak had been unnecessarily influenced by pressure from retailers and that the practice had served to keep their margins high.

D   EXCLUSIVE DEALING

A similar but slightly less permissive treatment is generally accorded to a supplier's practice of requiring his distributors not to deal in his competitors' products (*exclusive purchasing*). The corresponding practice by a distributor of requiring his suppliers not to supply to other distributors (*exclusive selling*) seldom occurs outside of exclusive distribution agreements (see p. 173) – except in respect of distributors' own brands, for which it is considered to be harmless (*Refusal to Supply 1970*).

European Union Practice

The conditions for exemption of exclusive purchasing agreements from the prohibition of Article 85(1) are similar – with the exception of references to a contract area – to those for exclusive distribution agreements which have been listed above. The exemption does not, however, apply if the agreement is for an indefinite duration or for a period of more than five years – with exceptions in that and other respects for sellers of beer and petrol (see Regulation 1984/83 and the associated Commission notice). As noted in section B above, certain restrictions occurring under agency and franchise agreements are also exempt.

Exclusive purchasing conditions are, however, prohibited if they foreclose a substantial part of a market (*Hoffman-La Roche 1975, Mars 1992*), and the same applies to loyalty rebates which tend to have the same effect (*Suiker Unie 1976*). In a later case, the offer of favourable delivery times to exclusive stockists in times of shortage has also been considered by the Commission to be an abuse of a dominant position (*British Gypsum 1988*).

United Kingdom Practice

Exclusive purchasing is not at present covered by the Restrictive Trade Practices Act 1976 unless it is collectively imposed by a group of suppliers, but it may be investigated under the Competition Act or the Fair Trading Act.

The practice has in some cases been voluntarily abandoned following an informal investigation under the Competition Act (for example, Kango Wolf in OFT guide) or after a formal investigation had found it to be anti-competitive (*Petter 1981*). The provision of large discounts to its own agents by a supplier of catering equipment was also stopped after it had been found to be anti-competitive (*Still 1982*). A condition imposed by a locally dominant newspaper that prevented newsagents from also handling free-sheet papers was found to be anti-competitive and was referred to the Monopolies and Mergers Commission. The Commission found the practice to be against the public interest but considered that the newspaper was entitled to protect itself against a selective attack by free-sheets which was aimed exclusively at its own readership (*Sheffield Newspapers 1982*). Restrictions imposed by Coca-Cola on the sales of competing products, revealed in the course of a monopoly investigation, were, however, deemed to be against the public interest (*Carbonated Drinks 1991*)

The Monopolies and Mergers Commission has been prepared to accept that exclusive buying can in some circumstances enhance competition. It was considered that competition in the promotion of a brand image and in the provision of spares and servicing might be keener when each distributor is committed to one supplier's products. Prices were in any case thought likely to be nearly uniform when the product is a homogenous commodity (*Liquefied Petroleum Gas 1981*).

An exclusive buying agreement with an agent or a franchisee may – as noted in section B above – be considered acceptable under some circumstances, but the practice was found to be against the public interest in a case in which it prevented franchised dealers from obtaining competing products which were readily available from other sources (*Car Parts 1982*).

It was noted in that case that the offer of discounts which are conditional upon maintaining a particular volume of sales or of stocks can have the effect of exclusive dealing, and in another case the abandonment of such practices and of unnecessarily long term contracts was recommended (*Metal Containers 1970*). Loyalty rebates can have a similar effect, but may be justifiable by cost savings. In a case in which the product was made to the customer's specification and loyalty rebates were not strictly related to cost savings, the practice was nevertheless considered to be justified as a means of obtaining savings from long production runs (*Flat Glass 1968*). The same effect often resulted from the provision at nominal rental of refrigerated cabinets for ice cream on the condition that they were used only for the supplier's products. That practice was, however, considered justifiable because sales might otherwise fall and competition and consumer choice might be reduced (*Ice Cream 1979 and 1994*).

E   FULL-LINE FORCING AND TIE-IN SALES

Under some circumstances, the competition authorities also seek to regulate the practice under which it is made a condition of supply that the purchaser buys the full range of a particular class of products (*full-line forcing*), and the practice under which it is made a condition that he also buys certain other products (*tie-in sales*). Their main concern is to prevent the use of market power over one product to acquire market power over another. The practices are consequently likely to escape regulation except when they are used by dominant firms for that purpose.

European Union Practice

Articles 85(1) and 86 of the Treaty of Rome both refer to the practice of:

> making the conclusion of contracts subject to acceptance by other parties of supplementary obligations which, by their nature or according to commercial usage, have no connection with the subject of such contracts.

Full-line forcing may be expected to escape the prohibition of Article 85(1) if it is part of a franchise, exclusive distribution or purchasing agreement which meets the requirements of the regulations referred to in sections B, C and D above. The practices which are specifically permitted under those regulations do not include tie-in sales, but that practice appears also to have escaped condemnation by the Commission under Article 85(1). The practices thus appear likely to be prohibited and to attract penalties only if they are employed by organisations occupying dominant positions under the terms of Article 86 (see section B of chapter 5).

Tying arrangements between brewers and their outlets are covered by the rules of Regulation No 1984/3, which is due to expire in 1997. The Commission propose to take account of the effectiveness of national rules in considering whether that regulation continues to be appropriate to conditions in the UK (Comp Rep 20 (1990)).

Among the practices at issue in the informal negotiations which led to the 1984 settlement between the Commission and IBM (see Comp Rep 14 (1985)) was IBM's refusal to sell the memory units of one of their computers separately from its central processing unit. Under less complex circumstances, Europe's largest manufacturers of power tools was fined for abuse of a dominant position in that they tied the supply of nails to the supply of cartridges (*Hilti 1988*) and a supplier of packaging machines was fined for tying the use of their cartons to the use of their machines (*Tetra Pak 1991*).

United Kingdom Practice

The possibility of prohibiting full-line forcing and tie-in sales was considered by an interdepartmental committee in 1979 (DTI 1979), as a result of which a general reference was made to the Monopolies and Mergers Commission under Section 83 of the Fair Trading Act. For the purpose of that reference the practices were taken to include:

> making the supply of goods or services available at prices or upon terms as to credit, discount or otherwise which are so disadvantageous as to be likely to deter that person or class of persons from acquiring those goods or services without acquiring other goods or services.

The Commission concluded that the practices are not always against the public interest, and that existing powers under the Fair Trading Act and the Competition Act were adequate for its regulation (*Full-Line Forcing 1981*). The practices were considered to be justified under franchise agreements under the circumstances described in section B above.

The distinction between justifiable and unjustifiable uses of tie-in sales had been illustrated by a case in which the rental terms for copying machines which had been imposed by a dominant supplier had included spares and servicing and the supply of a chemical referred to as 'toner'. The Commission found the control of spares and servicing to be justified by the need to protect the performance of the machines, but found that the policy regarding toner was against the public interest (*Reprographic Equipment 1976*). But that restriction was not considered objectionable some 14 years later, by which time the market share of the supplier had dropped from 90 per cent to 31 per cent (*Photocopiers 1991*). The supply of colour film only at prices which included a charge for processing had also been found to be against the public interest (*Colour Film 1966*) as was the tying of the sale of soft ice cream to the sale of hard ice cream (*Ice Cream 1979*). The Commission condemned an arrangement under which a hirer of an exhibition hall was compelled to employ only listed electricians (*Exhibition Halls 1990*). But it was considered to be an acceptable business practice to use the proceeds from the sales of caravans to subsidise the rentals of caravan sites and to reserve sites – 70 per cent of which were controlled by the caravan sellers in question - for buyers of their caravans (*Caravan Sites 1983*).

Part III
The Impact of Competition Policy

9 Trends: The Past and the Present

A INTRODUCTION

The review of the conduct of competition policy in Part II has been mainly concerned with the authorities' treatment of business practices in the course of the last 10 to 20 years. Competition policy has been presented in static terms – as though it had sprung into existence, fully developed, in the course of the 1970s. In fact, the conduct of competition policy has developed over a period of over 40 years, and it is still developing. A review of the impact of policy must therefore take account of earlier developments and of current trends.

Changes in the conduct of competition policy have occurred for a number of reasons. Its intellectual framework has been refined over the years, and there have been analytical innovations, some of which – such as the theory of contestable markets – remain a matter of controversy. Attitudes and beliefs – concerning, for example, freedom of contract and the advantages of size – have undergone radical change. Administrative institutions and procedures have evolved, sometimes haphazardly, and have adapted to the tasks and resource limitations which have faced them. Arbitrary criteria have been established to define jurisdiction and to distinguish between abusive and acceptable practices. Precedents have been established and overturned, and the predictability of the attitudes of the regulatory authorities to many business practices has increased.

The process of development has not, however, reached a stage at which further change is likely to be confined to relatively minor adjustments. There remain substantial areas of business behaviour, the regulatory treatment of which is still evolving, and on which evidence is incomplete or methods of analysis have yet to be established. The effectiveness and efficiency of existing methods of regulation are being questioned, and major institutional and procedural changes are under consideration.

As a background to the consideration of likely future developments in the concluding chapter, this chapter reviews the past development of competition policy, considers its direct impact on the behaviour and

185

structure of some of the industries with which it has been concerned and examines the extent of its indirect influence upon others.

B   THE DEVELOPMENT OF POLICY

United Kingdom Policy

The Common Law Origins

Textbooks on British competition law trace its origins to the thirteenth century in the development of the common law doctrine of *restraint of trade* (see, for example, Whish 1988, Chapter 2). Although that doctrine was founded upon the idea that there were public policy consequences of restraints upon trade, the interpretations put upon it in the late nineteenth century were concerned solely with reasonableness between the parties to an agreement. It was generally held that an agreement that was unreasonably in restraint of trade was unenforceable as between the parties to that agreement, but that third parties had no legitimate interest in the matter. Later decisions modified that interpretation, but at the time it seemed that the doctrine had ceased to have any relevance for competition policy.

The apparent collapse of the doctrine of the restraint of trade as an instrument of competition policy led in the United States to the passing of the Sherman Act (see section D of Chapter 1), but no British legislation on the subject was introduced until 1948. In the years following the First World War, policy action was discouraged by the belief that cartels and 'rationalisation' would be a means of preserving British industry in the face of the overcapacity which had been brought about by a collapse in demand, and of competition from large firms overseas. The reluctance to legislate on the matter was reinforced – or rationalised – by an appeal to the principle of freedom of contract. For example, the Committee on Restraint of Trade reported in 1930 that:

> We hold that the ordinary right of freedom of contract ought not to be withdrawn without some compelling reason. We do not regard the price maintenance system as free from disadvantages from the public point of view, but we are not satisfied that if a change in the law were made there is any reason to think that the interests of the public would be better served. (Quoted in *Collective Discrimination 1955*, Appendix 1)

Post-War Legislation

By 1944, however, the – by then extensive – cartelisation of British industry was being seen as an impediment to post-war reconstruction, and a government White Paper on employment proposed the creation of powers for the government to:

> inform themselves of the extent and effect of restrictive agreements and the activities of combines; and to take appropriate action to check practices which may bring advantages to the sectional producing interests, but work to the detriment of the country as a whole. (Cmd 6527)

The Monopolies and Restrictive Practices (Inquiry and Control) Act 1948 set up the Monopolies and Restrictive Practices Commission, to inquire on request into the effects upon the public interest of the activities of individual firms or combinations of firms which supplied 30 per cent or more of any market for goods. The Act did not specify any public interest criterion and did not mention competition. It gave powers to the (then) Board of Trade to make references and to apply remedies in response to adverse public interest findings. Early inquiries revealed the abuse of market power by monopolies, such as the excessive profits of the Anglo-Swedish match monopoly, and extensive cartelisation, among, for example, the suppliers of electric lamps and of cables. In nearly all of the 20 cases investigated by the Commission between 1948 and 1956, practices were revealed which were found to be against the public interest.

Restrictive Practices

In 1952, the Board of Trade called for a general inquiry into collective discrimination (exclusive dealing, collective boycotts, and the like) and the Commission's majority report on the subject recommended in 1955 that the collective imposition of such restrictions should be made a criminal offence, subject to exceptions to be adjudicated by an independent body. (*Collective Discrimination 1955*) The Government accepted instead the minority recommendation for the registration of agreements, followed by prohibition of all except those which were found not to be against the public interest. The Restrictive Trade Practices Act 1956 contained provisions similar to those of the current (1976) legislation (see section B of Chapter 2), except that it excluded information agreements and agreements relating to the supply of services, and that unregistered agreements were not made legally void.

The legislation had a dramatic impact. Following the second case brought before the Restrictive Practices Court in 1959, most parties to registrable agreements concluded that there was little prospect that the Court would allow them to continue, and that there was no point in incurring the great expense of attempting to defend them. Analysis of registrations indicated that some 50 to 60 per cent of UK manufacturing output had been subject to cartel restrictions (Elliott and Gribbin, 1977) but in the following ten years over 30 000 agreements were abandoned – only 39 of them as a result of judgements by the Court. There is evidence to suggest, however, that a substantial number of agreements – possibly 13 per cent of those existing before 1956 – continued to be operated in secret (Swann *et al.,* 1974).

Collectively enforced resale price maintenance was effectively eliminated by the 1956 Act, but individually enforced resale price maintenance was not brought under control until the passing of the Resale Prices Act 1964, under which it was prohibited unless exempted by order of the Court. Again, the impact was dramatic. Resale price maintenance is estimated to have applied to 20 to 25 per cent of consumers' expenditure in 1960 (Swann *et al.,* 1974), and by 1979 it applied only to books and medicines – covering less than 2 per cent of consumers' expenditure.

The restrictive practices legislation applied initially only to the suppliers of goods, but it was extended in 1976 to include the suppliers of services. There were exceptions, however, including agricultural marketing boards, transport operators, and virtually all professional services. In 1967, the Monopolies and Mergers Commission was asked to make a general inquiry into restrictions upon entry, upon the charging of fees, upon advertising, and upon other restrictive practices in the professions. The Commission concluded that the practices revealed by its inquiries were likely to be against the public interest, except under particular circumstances which for the most part did not generally arise (*Professional Services 1970*).

There followed a series of references to the Commission and negotiations by the Office of Fair Trading, resulting in the relaxation of restrictions on scale fees and advertising imposed by professional bodies on architects and surveyors, solicitors, accountants, stockbrokers, opticians and veterinary surgeons. A further review undertaken by the Office of Fair Trading in 1986 led to negotiations with professional associations concerning restrictions upon working with members of other professions in mixed practices.

An interdepartmental committee set up to review the legislation reported in 1988 that it was inflexible and slow, too often concerned with cases which are obviously harmless and not directed sufficiently at anti-competitive agreements. The scope for avoidance and evasion considerably weakens any deterrent effect the system has and enforcement powers are inadequate. The requirement to furnish insignificant agreements is not only wasteful of official resources but it imposes an excessive burden on firms. (DTI 1988)

On the advice of the committee the government announced its intention to introduce an effects-based system along the lines of Article 85. No such legislation has, however, been introduced.

Mergers

The pre-war belief that the concentration of firms into larger units would increase their efficiency continued to be held by many industrialists and politicians, well into the 1960s. Merger activity in the mid-1960s was at over five times its 1950 level, and was making a major contribution to the growth in concentration in manufacturing industry. In 1966, the Government set up the Industrial Reorganisation Corporation for the purpose of encouraging selected mergers. By that time, however, there was also a recognition that mergers could in some circumstances be harmful. The Monopolies and Mergers Act 1965 was framed on the assumption that although mergers were on the whole beneficial, a selected few should be investigated, and that those which could be shown to be damaging to the public interest should be prohibited.

In the early 1970s, evidence was mounting which showed that the expected efficiency gains from mergers had not materialised, and there was a change in the climate of opinion. In 1971 the Industrial Reorganisation Corporation was disbanded. The policy presumption in favour of mergers was challenged in 1978 by an interdepartmental committee which recommended that policy should be shifted to a neutral position (DTI, 1978). In the following years, however, the belief that most mergers are beneficial in themselves gave way to a belief that the merger process contributes to economic efficiency by establishing a 'market for corporate control' (see section A of Chapter 6). The proposed policy change was rejected, and the policy presumption in favour of mergers remains substantially as it was in the 1960s.

The Abuse of Market Power

The present functions of the Director-General of Fair Trading and of the Monopolies and Mergers Commission were defined in the Fair

Trading Act 1973. In respect of defined *monopoly situations,* this gave the Commission unlimited power to recommend remedies, and the Secretary of State unlimited powers to implement those or other remedies, but in respect only of matters which the Commission had found to be against the public interest. The remedies which were proposed involved the cessation of anti-competitive practices rather than divestments (with the single exception of the gas monopoly, the divestment of whose trading activities was recommended (*Gas 1993*) but not implemented). The Director-General was given few investigative powers, and no formal powers to make public interest judgements or initiate remedies – although in practice he acquired considerable powers in those respects from his function of negotiating undertakings. The scope for seeking undertakings in lieu of references was extended by the Deregulation and Contracting Out Act 1994 and the Director-General's powers in those respects were correspondingly enhanced.

In an attempt to provide for an effective but less cumbersome means of inquiry than was provided for by the Restrictive Practices and Fair Trading Acts, the Competition Act 1980 introduced a two-stage procedure under which the Director-General could undertake a formal inquiry into any anti-competitive practice by a qualifying firm and then decide whether to refer it to the Commission. The Deregulation Act 1994 removed the former of those stages of formal investigation but left the Director-General with the powers of investigation which the Competition Act had provided for that stage. Comparatively little formal use has been made of those powers, but they were widely used by the Director-General to bring about by persuasion the abandonment of practices which he considered to be anti-competitive.

Section 11 of the Competition Act also provided for inquiries by the Commission into the efficiency of public sector organisations (as described in section H of Chapter 2) and an extensive programme of such inquiries followed in the course of the 1980s. As the government's privatisation programme proceeded, the duties of regulating the various public utilities affected were assigned in turn of regulators appointed for the purpose, leaving the Commission with the role of determining appeals against the decisions of the regulators. The Director-General's powers in regard to anti-competitive practices were not formally altered, but in practice his office has since exercised a degree of cooperation with the regulators.

In 1992 in a consultative document, the Government noted that existing legislation provided a relatively weak deterrent against the abuse of market power and put forward three options, one of which would be a legal prohibition along the lines of Article 86 of the Treaty of Rome (DTI 1992). It was later announced that the Government had chosen instead the option of strengthening existing legislation by giving greater powers to the Director-General and introducing liability for civil damages – although it acknowledged that this would not fully address the issue of weak deterrence (DTI press notice of 14/4/93).

European Union Policy

Origins

The first measure of competition policy adopted on a European basis was incorporated in the Treaty of Paris, which set up the European Coal and Steel Community. This gave jurisdiction to a 'High Authority' to deal with restraints on competition within member states, whether or not they affected trade between member states. The Coal and Steel Community came into operation in 1953. Discussions among the six members of that community led to the signing of the Treaty of Rome, which came into effect in 1958. The formulation in that treaty of an effects-based system which made prohibited practices void unless exempted by the competition authority, owed a great deal to the outcome of the debate in West Germany which had led to the passing there of the Act Against Restraints of Competition (1957).

Restrictive Practices and the Abuse of a Dominant Position

Community competition policy did not, however, come fully into operation until after the ratification in 1962 of Regulation 17, governing regulatory procedures, including the procedures for notification and exemption described in section B of Chapter 3. In the following two years, the European Commission was fully engaged in processing upwards of 35 000 notifications, and its first formal decision was not issued until 1964. Substantial powers had been delegated to the Commission by the Council of the European Communities and in 1964 and the following few years, a firm legal foundation for its policies was established by the – mainly supportive – decisions of the European Court of Justice. The burden of dealing with notifications under Regulation 17 continued to dominate the Commission's activities for many years, however, and priority had to be given to the resolution of concerted practices under Article 85, particularly those relating to distribution and patent licensing. Action against the numerous cartels known to be operating in the Community was thus postponed, and it was not until 1969 that the Commission imposed fines upon a cartel. Action against abuse of a dominant position was similarly delayed, and the Commission's first formal decision under Article 86 was not taken until 1971.

The Commission's overload has since been substantially reduced by the introduction of regulations based upon established case law which have granted group exemptions to a range of agreements and practices and have thus reduced the need for notifications and case-by-case clearances. Simplified procedures including informal negotiations with firms and the issue of 'comfort letters' have also helped to reduce the Commission's backlog of notifications and complaints. Time became available to tackle horizontal restrictions and action was taken against cartels affecting quinine, dyestuffs, zinc, aluminum, parchment, glass, woodpulp and polypropylene and others. Article 85 cases continued to predominate, but some of the relatively few Article 86 cases – involving abuse of a dominant position – may have had more far-reaching consequences (such as the 1984 settlement with IBM, referred to in section E of Chapter 8).

State Aids and Restrictions on Public Utilities
Since the mid-1970s, the Commission has also mounted a progressively more determined attack upon state aids and other anticompetitive practices by the governments of member states. In the five years from 1977 to 1981 3 per cent of the 628 state aids examined by the Commission were ruled against or withdrawn; in the subsequent five years the percentage rose to 8 per cent of 1132 cases. Concealed subsidies in privatisation measures have been restrained, as in the case of the sale of the Rover Group to British Aerospace in 1988. State aids to agriculture are, however, exempt from regulation, except for products receiving Community support under the Common Agricultural Policy. Regulations concerning land transport and sea transport were introduced in 1968 and 1986, and in 1987 a regulation was issued which limited price-fixing in air transport, followed in 1989 by a ruling by the European Court of Justice enabling the Commission to prohibit price-fixing agreements applying to flights between member countries.

Mergers
Following a decision by the European Court that Article 86 could under some circumstances be used to regulate mergers, the Commission prepared a draft regulation in 1973 which would have given wider and better-defined powers. In response to opposition from Britain and other member states, further drafts were put forward in 1982, 1984, 1986,

1988 and the terms of a regulation were finally agreed in December 1989. However, the Commission was then already able to exert a substantial degree of informal influence over large cross-border merger proposals, and a number of mergers which had been cleared by national authorities had been re-examined and modified. The turnover thresholds above which the European Commission was given jurisdiction were higher than the Commission had wanted, but were made subject to review by the end of 1993. After extensive consultation involving the business community, legal practitioners and the member states, the Commission then concluded that, although there were strong arguments for lower thresholds, more experience should be gained before making any formal changes to the regulation. There is to be a further review in 1996.

C   THE DIRECT IMPACT ON INDUSTRIAL STRUCTURE AND BUSINESS BEHAVIOUR

Competition policy has been only one of many influences upon industrial structure and business behaviour, and there have been few attempts to isolate its contribution. Under these circumstances, the best that can be done is to examine past trends and consider what effects might plausibly be attributed to the direct impact of policy intervention.

Trends in the Structure of United Kingdom Industry

Industrial structure in Britain has been largely shaped by merger activity. In value terms the figures show a modest upward trend, on which is superimposed a series of very pronounced peaks of merger activity. As a percentage of total corporate assets, annual expenditures on acquisitions have varied from less than 1 per cent to over 8 per cent.

The first merger boom, which started at the end of the nineteenth century, brought together large numbers of firms into major horizontal combines in the textiles, chemicals, wallpaper, cement and soap industries. The second wave, in the 1920s, led to the creation of many of the firms which – on their own, or as components of subsequent mergers – now dominate British manufacturing industry, including ICI, GEC, Metal Box, Fison, Unilever and Cadbury-Fry. Merger activity increased again in the 1950s, reaching a peak in the 1960s, bringing AEI and English Electric under the control of GEC, and bringing about unions of other large firms to create new giants such as Cadbury Schweppes,

Rowntree Mackintosh, Allied Breweries, National Westminster and British Leyland. After subsiding to a comparatively low level in the early 1980s, spending on acquisitions began to rise again in 1984, and there was also a strong upward trend in divestments, transfers of subsidiaries and management buy-outs. Large, bitterly contested bids (such as the Guinness bid for Distillers) became more common, as did conglomerate divestments of product ranges to former rivals (such as Hansons's sale of Courage to Elders) or to the incumbent management.

The two pre-war merger waves may have been motivated as much by the desire to achieve scale economies and to reap the advantages of nationwide marketing, as by the desire to gain market power. They nevertheless resulted in considerable accretions of market power in certain industries which, together with the formation of cartels and the erection of barriers against imports, afforded the firms concerned opportunities to protect themselves against competition. The post-war merger boom was probably encouraged for a time by the passing of the Restrictive Practices Act, as a result of which cartels and price rings were virtually prohibited, leaving mergers as an unregulated alternative means of limiting competition in the early 1960s. In the second half of the 1960s, however, the newly instituted mergers legislation began to have a slight restraining influence. Ten mergers were referred to the Monopolies and Mergers Commission, of which four were found to be against the public interest, and two were abandoned (including Unilever/United Breweries, which was abandoned after being found not to be against the public interest). But a more important influence arose from the activities of the Industrial Reorganisation Corporation during that period in either providing financial support for mergers, or ensuring that they were not referred to the Commission. The direction of public policy during this period was uncertain, and its net effect was probably again to encourage mergers.

In the early 1970s there were signs that merger policy was beginning to bite. Some large horizontal mergers, such as Boots/Glaxo, were prohibited and it became evident that the Commission was becoming sceptical of claims that scale economies would necessarily contribute to efficiency. In the course of the 1970s, some 45 mergers were referred (some 2–3 per cent of those qualifying), of which 12 were found to be against the public interest and 16 were abandoned before inquiries were completed. It gradually became clear that – in the absence of mitigating factors such as entry prospects – there was a risk that any large merger creating combined market shares much in excess of 40 per cent might be prohibited. That risk, together with the costs of failure (running, perhaps into tens of £millions) must be presumed to have been a deterrent to many of those contemplating such mergers, as well as prompting the abandonment of some of those which were referred.

In the course of the 1970s and the first half of the 1980s, the British competition authorities also became involved in a number of contested mergers which did not raise significant competition issues (such as those involving Harrods and Sothebys). The threat of a merger reference came to be used by target managements as a means of defence, and the Commission frequently had to adjudicate between competing management claims. In retrospect, this can probably now be dismissed as a confused and inconclusive episode.

The 1980s saw a growth in the practice of incorporating divestiture and other undertakings into merger proposals in order to reduce their market power implications and thereby to avoid a merger reference. The process of informal clearance by consultation with the Office of Fair Trading thereby assumed increasing importance, as compared with the formal procedures of the Monopolies and Mergers Commission. Similar undertakings have increasingly become a feature of informal negotiations with the European Commission, prior notification to whom has become normal practice for mergers with a possible Community dimension.

Market concentration (as measured, for example, by the total share of a market supplied by the five largest suppliers) rose markedly on average in the 1950s and 1960s, but levelled off and declined in the 1970s and 1980s.

Underlying Influences

Important influences besides that of competition policy were at work, and many of the changes of industrial structure which have been reviewed may have originated from motives other than a desire to restrict competition. The integration of local soap manufacturers and the marketing of the product under national brand names, for example, seems to have occurred in response to scale economies available at the time, and to a demand for a product which could be relied upon not to cause skin damage. In a number of other British industries, developments in technology and marketing were a force for change: indeed the fact that increases in concentration tended to occur in the same industries in other industrialised economies suggests that they were the main driving force. Thus it is possible that the creation of monopolies may at first have occurred in response to economic forces, and that the opportunities for exploitation which they provided may not have been realised until later.

Subsequent developments in technology and marketing may explain why the growth in concentration which occurred in the first half of the century and beyond did not persist into the 1970s and 1980s. Changes in technology have in the latter period often tended to reduce scale economies. Standardisation (as in the case of petrol) and the development of retailers' 'own brands' have reduced the importance of suppliers' brands. There has also been a growing awareness that the technical advantages of large-scale operation could be offset by disadvantages in other respects. Very large firms had been found to experience special difficulties in managing industrial relations and in responding to changing market conditions. E.F. Schumacher's dictum that 'small is beautiful' has found its way into corporate thinking.

Although nationwide monopolies remain, there has also been a progressive reduction in their market power. Competition from imports has made a very substantial impact. In the 1960s tariffs fell steeply on imports from all sources, and in the 1970s tariff barriers and quantitative restrictions upon imports from other members of the European Community were abolished altogether. There are now few manufacturing sectors in which imports do not make a significant contribution to competition. The market power of large British-owned firms has also been eroded by competition from foreign firms operating in the United Kingdom, which accounted by 1988 for some 20 per cent of British manufacturing output.

Intervention in the Affairs of Dominant Firms

It is difficult, therefore, to isolate the contribution which the regulatory authorities have made to the general lowering of barriers to competition which has occurred. An indication can, however, be obtained by tracing the history of their intervention into the affairs of dominant firms.

British markets which, by the 1950s, had come to be dominated by small groups of large firms included the national markets for glass, plasterboard, matches, electric cables, detergents, petrol and beer. The behaviour of dominant firms in most of those markets has been investigated from time to time by the competition authorities, and there has been official intervention on a number of occasions to prohibit acquisitions which those firms had proposed or to change some of their business practices. Those interventions, and their backgrounds, may be summarised as follows.

Glass

Pilkington Brothers was founded in 1826 as the St Helens Crown Glass Company. By 1905, it was the sole British manufacturer of plate glass and its only domestic competitor in the supply of sheet glass was Chance Brothers. In 1936 the two companies, which had for some years operated pricing agreements, set up a market-sharing agreement for cast glass, and by 1945, Chance had become a subsidiary of Pilkington. Domestic competition was thereby eliminated, and overseas competition was limited by a number of market-sharing and price-fixing agreements with continental manufacturers and with British glass merchants. In 1929, Pilkington and Triplex formed a joint company for the manufacture of safety glass, and Pilkington had acquired a controlling interest in Triplex by 1965 and full ownership by 1972 – eliminating thereby all domestic competition in that market.

A Monopolies Commission report in 1968 approved the acquisition of Triplex and expressed confidence that Pilkington would not abuse its monopoly power (*Flat Glass 1968*), but a subsequent report opposed Pilkington's proposed acquisition of the only UK supplier of mass-produced lenses (*Pilkington/UKO 1977*). Pilkington announced in 1957 that it had abandoned its price-fixing arrangements with British glass merchants, but admitted in 1988 that it had operated a price-fixing arrangement for double glazing units between 1978 and 1984. In November 1990 the Restrictive Practices Court ruled that 12 price-fixing agreements covering stock float glass, toughened, laminated and silvered glass were against the public interest, and accepted undertakings from Pilkington and 40 other companies not to enforce such agreements.

Plasterboard

British Plasterboard was founded in 1917, and had by 1945 acquired most of the British capacity for the production of plasterboard and of its raw materials. In 1967 and 1968 it acquired all remaining British plasterboard manufacturing capacity from its two competitors. Neither acquisition was referred to the Monopolies Commission but a monopoly reference was made in 1972, in response to which the Commission offered no criticism of the way in which the company's monopoly position had been established, but expressed doubts about its efficiency and made recommendations as a result of which British Plasterboard eventually undertook in 1977 to abandon its system of uniform delivered prices (*Plasterboard 1974*). On Britain's entry into the European Community in 1973, British Plasterboard announced the abandonment of restrictions upon imports from its associates in the Community, which they regarded as invalid under the Treaty of Rome. In 1988, however, the company was fined £2 million by the European Commission for operating a fidelity payments scheme and offering favourable delivery times to exclusive stockists, following the use by the Commission of their entry powers to get evidence of the obstruction of imports. In 1990 the Monopolies and Mergers Commission noted that, mainly as a result of the entry of Redland into the market, British Plasterboard's share of the market had fallen from 97 per cent to less than 75 per cent, and that there was vigorous price competition. On the Commission's recommendation, the 1977 undertakings concerning delivered prices were lifted (*Plasterboard 1990*).

Matches

In 1861, Bryant and May, then UK agents of a Swedish company, started the manufacture under licence of safety matches. By the 1920s, all the other British match producers had been absorbed either into Bryant and May or into J. John Masters, which was by then under the control of Swedish Match. In 1927 Bryant and May and Masters combined to form the British Match Corporation, a 33 per cent shareholding in which went to Swedish Match. Agreements were set up for the sharing of world markets, and the monopoly was further protected by restrictions on the supply of match-making machinery.

A Monopolies Commission report (*Matches 1953*) found those arrangements to be against the public interest, and recommended the ending of restrictions on the supply of match-making machinery, but not of most of the other agreements. The report led to a renegotiation of those agreements but the main links between Swedish Match and the British Match Corporation remained. In 1973 British Match acquired Wilkinson Sword, and between 1978 and 1980 Alleghany International (an American domestic appliance manufacturer) acquired the Wilkinson Match combine including all of the Swedish Match holding – although Masters remained under the day-to-day control of Swedish Match as their UK agent. In 1987, Alleghany agreed to sell all of Wilkinson Match to Swedish Match. The effect was to give the combined company total control of 99 per cent of match manufacture, 82 per cent of match distribution, and 42 per cent of the sales of disposable lighters, in the UK. It was cleared by the Monopolies and Mergers Commission (*Swedish Match/Alleghany 1987*). A 1992 report revealed profit rates on capital employed of over 200 per cent and recommended price control in order to prevent Bryant and May from earning excessive profits in the future. (*Matches 1992*).

Electric Cable

In 1945, the two largest British electric cable manufacturers merged to form British Insulated Cables Ltd (BICC), accounting for around 25 per cent of British production of insulated wires and cables, and with interests in copper refining and electrical construction. BICC became the leading member of the Cable Makers' Association which operated various market-sharing and price-fixing schemes. In 1952, those schemes were abandoned on the recommendation of the Monopolies Commission (*Insulated Wires and Cables 1952*).

Between 1955 and 1977 there were about a dozen further mergers and BICC's share of UK production rose to 35 per cent. Among those mergers, BICC's acquisition of Pyrotenax, which gave it a 90 per cent share of the UK market for mineral insulated cables was referred to the Monopolies and Mergers Commission and was cleared on the understanding that the resulting cost savings would be used to expand sales and reduce prices, and that BICC would not operate a number of specified anti-competitive practices. (An undertaking then given to supply other manufacturers was unexpectedly taken up by GEC, giving it an advantage in other markets which has since been the subject of dispute.) The Commission found in 1979 that BICC's monopoly did not operate against the public interest, but that with three other suppliers, BICC had been operating an unregistered restrictive agreement concerning supplies of cable to the Post Office (*Insulated Wires and Cables 1979*). In an out of court settlement the companies agreed to pay the Post Office £9 million in compensation.

Detergents

Lever Brothers (now Unilever) started soap manufacture in 1885 and pioneered the marketing of soap in Britain under national brand names. By 1920, having acquired a number of its former competitors, Lever became UK market leader. Under various market sharing arrangements with Lever, ICI and Shell agreed not to enter the detergent market, but those arrangements had been abandoned by the early 1950s. Procter and Gamble, a successful United States soap producer, made a substantial entry into the British market following its acquisition of Thomas Hedley in 1930. By the early 1960s the two firms were supplying over 90 per cent of the British household detergents market.

In 1963 that situation was referred to the Monopolies Commission who reported that there was little price competition, that prices were unnecessarily high, and that entry was being deterred by excessive advertising expenditures. The Commission recommended that the companies should reduce their advertising expenditures by at least 40 per cent and their selling prices by around 20 per cent (*Household Detergents 1966*). Its recommendations were not accepted. The companies undertook instead to introduce new low-priced brands backed by relatively low-cost promotions. Those undertakings were amended and eventually abandoned in the 1970s in view of the increased buying power of the supermarket groups and of competition from their own brands. Advertising expenditures were, however, generally reduced in the 1970s and some price competition emerged, but the combined market share of the two companies declined by less than 8 per cent between 1964 and 1983.

Petrol

In 1964 the three leading suppliers, Shell/BP, Esso and Regent (now Texaco) supplied over 90 per cent of the UK petrol market and controlled 85 per cent of the retail sites by virtue either of ownership or of exclusive supply contracts. The Monopolies Commission inquiry at that time was, however, confined by its terms of reference to the question of the control of the retail outlets. As a result of their report (*Petrol 1965*), the companies undertook to restrict the durations of exclusive supply agreements to five years, renewable annually thereafter. (Two restraint of trade cases at about the same time established that long-term agreements for the supply of petrol were unreasonable.) The companies also undertook to restrict the acquisition of further petrol stations, but were later released from that undertaking. Between 1964 and 1979, new suppliers had captured about a quarter of the market and the leading suppliers' shares of the market and of the number of controlled outlets dropped to below 66 per cent.

As the result of a further inquiry, the Commission found that the extent of the ownership of outlets was not then against the public interest, but suggested that the situation be kept under review by the Director-General of Fair Trading (*Petrol 1979*). In 1983 the European Commission issued a block exemption for exclusive purchase agreements with petrol stations lasting for up to ten years or for the duration of a tenancy if longer. In June 1988 a House of Commons Select Committee announced that it had found prima facie evidence of resale price maintenance of petrol stations, and on its recommendation a further monopoly reference was made. The report of that inquiry noted that almost all retail outlets were still tied to suppliers, either by ownership or by exclusive supply agreements, but that there was no evidence of price collusion or of excessive profits (*Petrol 1990*). The subsequent entry of supermarkets into petrol retailing has since made it possible to buy petrol at lower prices than those charged by the tied outlets.

Beer

As for petrol, the market for beer is characterised by extensive control of retail outlets by suppliers. (In the case of beer, however, the origins of that control lie in the operation in the nineteenth century of a restrictive licensing system intended to prevent 'social abuse'.) The merger boom of the 1960s brought together a number of regional brewers to form 'the big six' (Bass, Allied, Whitbread, Watney, Courage and Scottish and Newcastle) who by 1969 supplied 68 per cent of the UK market, and owned about 50 per cent of all on-licences (outlets – mainly public houses – licensed to sell beer for consumption on the premises which in total account for over 85 per cent of UK beer sales). The brewers imposed 'ties' and exclusive purchasing arrangements upon those outlets, which the Monopolies Commission found in 1969 to be against the public interest (*Beer 1969*). The Commission's recommendation that the licensing laws should be relaxed was not implemented. No other remedies were proposed.

Between 1968 and 1972, there were some 15 further mergers involving the 'big six', none of which were referred to the Commission (although a projected merger between Unilever and Allied Breweries was abandoned after it had been referred and the Commission had cleared it). Three mergers involving Scottish and Newcastle have since been referred to the Commission, the first of which was abandoned, the second was cleared and the third (with Elders IXL) was stopped. The acquisitions of Courage, first by Imperial, then by Hanson, and then by Elders in 1986, were not referred. Between 1967 and 1986 the proportion of on-licences owned by brewers had fallen from 78 per cent to 56 per cent, but the domination of the 'big six' had increased to the point where they accounted for 75 per cent both of UK beer production and of brewer-owned premises.

Following a further reference in 1986, the Monopolies and Mergers Commission found there to be a complex monopoly situation which operated against the public interest by overcharging and restricting consumer choice (*Beer 1989*). The resulting *Beer Orders* required each brewer to untie half of all of its pubs in excess of 2000, either by sale or letting; to allow tied pubs to sell at least one of its competitors' beers, and to allow loan-ties to be terminated without penalty. In 1990 a merger between two of the 'big six', which was expected to lead to a market share of around 40 per cent for all beer and 47 per cent for lager, was allowed, subject to undertakings designed to reduce the extent of local monopolies and put an eventual end to exclusive purchasing ties. (*Elders/Grand Met 1990*). The then Secretary of State announced, however, that further increases in concentration would be unwelcome unless accompanied by major weakening of vertical links between brewing and retailing (DTI Press notice 16/10/90).

The Consequences of Intervention

The limited direct impact of the above interventions upon the markets in question can be ascribed in part to limitations upon the authorities' powers and resources. Many of the dominant firms concerned had achieved dominance before the present competition authorities existed, or before they had acquired their present powers of intervention. Effective action concerning existing monopolies must thereafter have been difficult to envisage. Any attempt to reduce the market power of the dominant firms by forced divestiture could have created industrial disruption on an incalculable scale, and systematic regulation of their commercial behaviour would in many cases have required a thoroughness of investigation and monitoring for which sufficient resources were not available. Action could be taken against overt cartels – and was taken, with great effect – but little could be done about the secret operation of cartels and other restrictive practices.

After 1965, however, powers were available to prevent dominant firms from augmenting their market power by mergers, but only limited use was made of them. The non-reference of many mergers, and the permissive attitude adopted towards many of those which were referred may have seemed justifiable on several grounds. In some cases the dominant firm was already so powerful that the further acquisitions which were proposed would make little difference. In other cases the authorities appear to have been influenced by the argument that large-scale operations were necessary in order to enable British firms to compete with overseas suppliers. In general, there was a disposition to accept estimates of efficiency gains and assurances of good behaviour, in the absence of convincing grounds for scepticism.

It would thus appear that, for a variety of reasons, the British competition authorities did not exert a decisive influence upon the major markets supplied by dominant firms. They may, nevertheless, have had an important indirect influence upon those and other markets. The mere risk of investigation may have deterred some of the largest companies from seeking to increase their market power by merger. Business practices which created artificial barriers to entry may also have been deterred by the risk of discovery and of investigations under which they might be condemned. It may have become clear to businessmen in large corporations that the competition authorities considered that the possession of market power carried with it a special obligation to refrain from anti-competitive and exploitative behaviour. The assurances of good behaviour that were given to the Commission may not always have been fully carried out, but they may have had a restraining influence on the corporate policy of those that gave them, and of others.

By its nature, the extent of such indirect influence is impossible to measure. It is likely, however, to depend upon the transparency and consistency of the decisions of the regulatory authorities. A review of that aspect of the conduct of competition policy may therefore lead to an impressionistic assessment of its true impact.

D TRANSPARENCY, CONSISTENCY AND EFFICIENCY

Most of the work of the regulatory authorities is hidden from view, and most of their decisions are taken for reasons which are not published. This is necessarily true of the confidential advice which is given to individual businessmen by the Office of Fair Trading and the Competition Directorate of the European Commission. It is also true to a varying extent of their discretionary interpretation of published rules and guidelines. Only a small fraction of cases which meet the statutory conditions for reference to the Monopolies and Mergers Commission are in fact referred, and the criteria for selection have not been revealed. (Published guidelines contain little beyond a summary of the legislation and a listing of the considerations which are taken into account.) The same applies to the criteria by which agreements which are considered to be of minor economic significance escape reference to the Restrictive Practices Court. Community practice also lacks total transparency – concerning, for example, the criteria for establishing the existence of a dominant position – although some broad quantitative guidelines have been issued in that case, and the Community's regulations and guidelines tend generally to be reasonably specific.

Lack of transparency in those respects may limit the indirect impact of competition policy if it engenders uncertainty concerning the circumstances under which the authorities are likely to intervene. If that uncertainty were total, intervention by the authorities would be universally regarded as an unpredictable business risk: but that is not of course the case. Managements of leading firms may be certain that any overt action to enhance or exploit their market power will attract the attention of the authorities, and the existence of practically any form of competition policy may thus be expected to exert a substantial indirect influence on their business conduct. It is the impact of policy upon firms with substantial, but not overwhelming, market power which is most uncertain.

Regularities in the past behaviour of the regulatory authorities reduce the area of uncertainty, however, and so contribute to the indirect impact of policy. Consistency of treatment can thus be at least a partial substitute for transparency. As the previous chapters have demonstrated, the pursuit of broadly similar objectives and methods of analysis has, in many areas of business conduct, led to reasonably consistent patterns of published decisions. Such logical aberrations as have occurred have been generally recognised, and the temporary uncertainties which they produced have tended to diminish under the impact of subsequent cases.

Policy cannot be conducted solely on the basis of logic, however: arbitrary distinctions have to be drawn, and coordination is then essential to consistency. The cases which have been reviewed in Part II of this book exhibit a number of deficiencies in this respect. One example is the use of market share criteria in cases where there are product substitutes or where the relevant market is a local one. The choice of market definition in such cases is necessarily arbitrary, and some agreement is needed concerning the basis for drawing a line. The decision whether to include a potential substitute could, for example, be based upon a chosen percentage by which a given price increase would alter customer choice in favour of that substitute (as has been proposed in the US Justice Department's merger guidelines, referred to in section A of Chapter 5). There is no sign that the British or the Community authorities have agreed on such a criterion, although there are some indications that the Community authorities accept the underlying methodology.

A further deficiency concerns the criteria by which conduct deemed to be anti-competitive is distinguished from conduct which is regarded as a legitimate means of seeking a competitive advantage. The use of predatory pricing, for example, can be established objectively where documentary proof of intent is available, but otherwise it cannot consistently be distinguished from competitive pricing except on an arbitrary basis. The Areeda-Turner rules use marginal or average variable costs for that purpose, but the Community authorities have rejected those rules without proposing an alternative; and as a result, it is imposs-

ible for a businessman to know where he stands. The British authorities have in the past created similar uncertainties concerning the use
of advertising as an entry barrier by ruling certain levels of advertising to be excessive without stipulating any effects-based criterion (relating, for example, to the effect on the market share needed for successful
entry).

The attitude of the competition authorities to excessive pricing might,
however, be considered to be the most important area of uncertainty.
It raises an important issue because it faces the directors of leading
firms with a direct conflict between their duties to shareholders and
their public interest obligations. (That issue has from time to time been
clouded by the consideration that excessive pricing may attract new
entry, but it is a clear-cut issue in the case of a natural monopoly, or
in a case in which entry prospects are remote.) Its importance has
been increased by the privatisation of public utilities and by the need
within the Community for coordination of their pricing policies so that
competition among their customers is not distorted. Those issues have
been recognised by the UK competition authorities and substantial
progress has been made toward the establishment of an acceptable
methodology.

Thus, although there are very considerable areas of business conduct which have been decisively affected by the indirect influence of
competition policy, there are also a number of important areas where
its influence has been far from decisive. In those areas, intervention
by the authorities has the character of a business risk, which cannot be
resolved except by an expensive case-by-case process of trial and error. In any assessment of the impact of policy upon the economy, therefore, the burden of cost and uncertainty which it has placed upon business
has to be set against the benefits which it has conferred in promoting
competition.

Effectiveness in promoting competition is in any case not the only
criterion by which competition policy is to be judged. The improvements in allocative efficiency which it thereby achieves have to be
balanced against possible losses in productive efficiency – including,
or in addition to, the costs which its procedures impose upon business.

Some of its procedures appear, in fact, to have achieved effectiveness largely by virtue of their inefficiency. The effectiveness of the
Restrictive Practices Act in putting an end to a wide range of agreements in manufacturing owed much to the high cost of defending them
in court, and to uncertainties about the way in which the Act would be
interpreted. As a result, comparatively few cases have come before the

Court, and a comprehensive and up-to-date body of case law has not been developed. The legislation nevertheless requires the continued notification and registration of large numbers of agreements, most of which are harmless. Adjudication, where it is required, rests with the Office of Fair Trading, and may involve firms in protracted negotiations concerning restrictions considered by the Office to be objectionable. The Office does not publish its reasons for individual decisions, and its published guide to the legislation deals with major issues in only the most general of terms. Criteria for the treatment of joint ventures and of buying groups, for example, are each dealt with in a few sentences. The regulatory procedure has thus imposed substantial costs upon business in terms both of administrative effort and of uncertainty, and may have deterred the setting up of generally advantageous agreements. Restrictive practices in the professions, by contrast, have been tackled largely by negotiations with professional associations; a procedure which has been very slow in getting results, but which has avoided placing comparable burdens upon businesses, and which has produced explicit codes of behaviour.

In their early stages in particular, the procedures by which the EU has dealt with concerted practices have also subjected businesses to substantial costs and uncertainties, and there is still a very large backlog of notified agreements on which rulings are awaited. The publication of block exemptions has greatly reduced the areas of delay and uncertainty, however, and there is now a wide range of activities for which businessmen have only to follow reasonably explicit rules in order to be confident that the authorities will not intervene.

E CONCLUSIONS

Although the evidence which has been reviewed in this chapter does not justify a confident assessment of the impact of competition policy, some tentative conclusions can be drawn. Among the least controversial must be the observation that the direct effects of the formal decisions of the regulatory authorities upon the firms which they have investigated amount in total to, at most, a minor influence upon the economy. The relatively small number of such decisions – fewer than 20 a year each by the European Commission and the Monopolies and Mergers Commission – would on its own justify such a conclusion. The vastly more numerous informal contacts which have taken place between firms and the regulatory authorities must also be assumed to have had a very limited total impact in view of the relatively insignificant numbers of staff involved. Thus if it is to be concluded that competition policy has had a significant influence upon the economy, that influence must have arisen from the effect of the decisions of the authorities upon the behaviour of businessmen at large.

Surprisingly, however, there is no hard evidence concerning the perceptions of businessmen as to the conduct which the regulatory authorities are likely to find acceptable or unacceptable. The lack of published market research on that question might indeed be considered to be among the most remarkable aspects of the conduct of competition policy. In the absence of such evidence, assessment must depend upon an evaluation of the strength of the signals which the authorities have transmitted. On that question, however, the indications are mixed. On some practices such as retail price maintenance there has been a clear negative signal, masked only very slightly by 'noise'. On other practices, the signal is either very weak in itself or is heavily masked by the noise of apparently conflicting decisions.

Major contributions to improvements in the signal-to-noise ratio have come from the Community's block exemption regulations. (The power which is reserved to withdraw those exemptions in selected cases might be considered to cause uncertainty, but in practice it probably reduces uncertainty by allowing little scope for semantic devices to circumvent policy intentions.) An exclusive dealing agreement which is drafted in accordance with the appropriate regulation, for example, is virtually certain of approval. The process by which those regulations have evolved has been very slow, however, and there are still gaps which remain to be filled. That process has, as yet, no counterpart in British practice.

Explanatory notices and guidelines issued by the European Commission have made further contributions – as, to a lesser extent, have those issued by the British authorities. The regulations and guidelines which have been issued by the European Commission have for the most part followed the examples and precedents established by the published decisions of the regulatory authorities. Despite their comparatively minor direct impact, those decisions have thus been the ultimate source of the signals which have gone out to businessmen – and of the noise which has accompanied them.

The ultimate impact of competition policy upon the economy must depend, however, upon the quality of the signals conveyed, as well as their strength. Quality has been determined by the skill and accuracy with which the authorities have balanced economic gains and losses in reaching their decisions. The few independent attempts which have been made to assess the quality of the authorities' decisions have for the most part been inconclusive or unconvincing, and it is doubtful whether an outsider can provide a reliable answer. In some of the cases which have been reviewed in Part II, it appears that conclusions have been arrived at intuitively rather than by the collection and analysis of evidence. In some others, the connection between the evidence and the conclusion is not convincingly explained. Such observations raise doubts, but do not establish whether other methods could have yielded more reliable conclusions.

It seems beyond doubt, however, that influences other than competition policy have been more important, notably the increase in competition from abroad. The following assessment by the then Director-General of Fair Trading makes that point:

> Indeed, the power of international trade as a solvent of cartels and a disarmer of monopolies should not be underrated. Would that competition authorities were always as effective. Three very different examples will illustrate its power. The **cement cartel** survived two examinations by the Restrictive Practices Court but was finally abandoned after several decades, in the face of imports from Greece and Spain, after those countries had joined the European Community. The **plasterboard monopoly** survived for many years after examination by the Monopolies and Mergers Commission, thanks to its tight hold on United Kingdom sources of gypsum, but it is now under challenge from a British company obtaining supplies of gypsum from elsewhere in the Community. And the **Stock Exchange**, having been forced to adapt to the globalisation of securities trading, bears little relationship to the body whose restrictive rule-book I challenged under the Restrictive Practices Act. (DGFT, 1988)

Such developments lend support to the argument of the Austrian and Chicago Schools (referred to in section B of Chapter 1) that, given effective action to remove entry barriers, intervention by the competition authorities is largely unnecessary. There has indeed been pressure from industrial lobbies to limit the activities of the competition authorities on the grounds that overseas competition has already made their interventions unnecessary. The Director-General of Fair Trading has replied that he does take account of overseas competition in his decisions and recommendations, but that many markets remain which are essentially domestic in character (DGFT, 1988).

It may reasonably be concluded that the regulatory authorities have on balance made a positive contribution to the removal of obstacles to competition over a period during which other favourable influences have probably been more important. They have done so, however, at a substantial cost to businessmen in terms of the disruption caused by their investigations and – more importantly – of the uncertainties which their activities have created. There still remain substantial areas of business activity concerning which intervention by the competition authorities has to be considered to be in the nature of an unpredictable business risk. Much remains to be done to reduce such uncertainties by the development and refinement of procedures and methods of analysis, and above all by more effective communication with the business world. There is little to suggest, however, that the dissatisfaction among businessmen with the activities of the competition authorities is likely to amount to a consensus that competition policy should be abolished. It will be required to develop its understanding of business and to adapt to changing circumstances, but it is here to stay.

10 The Future

A INTRODUCTION

Competition policy, as it affects British businessmen, has in some respects achieved maturity. Over a substantial range of business practices, the rules are well established and are consistently enforced without imposing unnecessary burdens. But uncertainties remain concerning the likely attitudes of the authorities to some business practices, and there remains a further range of practices over which competition policy exerts little deterrent influence. It would seem reasonable to expect long-term progress in those respects, but short-term trends have become difficult to discern, and some periods of instability may intervene before maturity is fully achieved.

B DEVELOPMENT OF THE RULES

Although the concept of legal precedent plays no formal part in the bulk of British domestic competition policy, there has in recent years been a growing recognition of the need for consistent decision making. The European Commission has long been committed to the gradual development, through its decisions, of a consistent body of rules, and Britain's domestic authorities may now be expected to follow suit. Domestic rules are likely to influence and be influenced by EU regulations and precedents, and eventually to converge with them.

The most significant refinement in the rules would be an improvement in the practice of balancing the gains from promoting competition against any consequent losses in productive efficiency. Decisions made on the presumption that competition effects always predominate can differ markedly from decisions made on the opposite presumption. Further empirical work to determine what actually happens under different circumstances may lead to more rational decisions, as well as reducing the instability which can be generated by intuition-based changes of presumption. Progress in this direction may result, for example, from analyses of the circumstances under which mergers have yielded performance benefits, and from surveys of consumers' reactions to restraints placed by suppliers on retailers. It is hard to envisage the indefinite continuation of the present situation under which no check is made upon any of the judgements upon such matters which have been made by the regulatory authorities.

There is also scope for refinement of the rules governing the regulation of natural monopolies such as the privatised public utilities. In the short- to medium-term there is scope for further development of pricing policies relating to the concept of an acceptable rate of return but, if the incentive for productive efficiency is not to be sacrificed, there may in the longer-term be a need to develop an acceptable cost-related approach, accompanied by efficiency audits. The problem of meeting the information requirements necessary for the success of such an approach may, however, delay progress along that path.

Improved understanding may lead to stabler and more rational rules, but there is likely to be a continuing need to draw arbitrary distinctions concerning, for example, practices which are harmful only when carried to extremes. Arbitrary decisions can be damaging to business confidence, but arbitrary rules need not be. Specific criteria will probably be developed and promulgated, along the lines of the US Department of Justice's *five per cent* test for market definition and the Areeda-Turner criterion for predatory pricing.

A resolution is also to be expected of the conflict between the need for transparency of decision-making and the savings obtainable by enabling firms to obtain informal guidance in order to avoid formal proceedings. Some sacrifice of commercial confidentiality may be needed in order to provide general access to such guidance.

C ENFORCEMENT

The transition of domestic competition policy from a case-by-case approach to the development of a system of rules is likely to be accompanied by the introduction of effective powers of detection and penalties for breaches of those rules. This could occur by one of several possible routes. A proposal to introduce a legal prohibition of restrictive practices, along the lines of Article 85 of the Treaty, has long been accepted but not implemented, and a legal prohibition of monopoly abuse along the lines of Article 86 has more recently been considered but rejected. It is widely accepted that, as matters stand, the deterrent effect of British competition law is unacceptably weak, giving an unfair advantage to those who are willing and able to evade it.

One possible route toward a remedy would be the enforcement of

EU law in the British courts. Where a *community dimension* can be established, it is already open to complainants to seek remedies in the British Courts under Articles 85 and 86, but costs and uncertainties have deterred most complainants from that course of action. Unlike some of its continental counterparts, the Office of Fair Trading is not at present empowered to use the British courts in that way. If it were given such powers and the corresponding powers of investigation, the Office's effectiveness, and the deterrent effects of its activities would be greatly increased. This would, however, mean that the opportunities for case-by-case intervention by the Secretary of State would correspondingly be curbed. That consideration must be regarded however as an obstacle to such a development rather than a disadvantage. The main disadvantage of that route arises from the lack of the relevant intellectual disciplines among the British judiciary, and this has led to a suggestion that the Monopolies and Mergers Commission be constituted as a special court for that purpose.

Whatever route is eventually chosen, however, eventual convergence with European Union practice in this respect also, must be considered inevitable.

D ADMINISTRATION AND ACCOUNTABILITY

The institutional system which administers British competition policy is anomalous by international standards and there have been numerous calls for change. The reform most frequently advocated is the replacement of the Office of Fair Trading and the Monopolies Commission by a single competition authority, as recommended by the House of Commons Trade and Industry Committee. (House of Commons 1995)

The case for introducing such changes depends mainly upon the perceived performance of the institutions concerned. To the extent that their decisions are generally accepted as being impartial, consistent, and well-judged in the public interest, a plausible case can be made against any substantial change. The skills acquired over the years in managing under the existing regime would be lost, and the process of adjustment to new institutional arrangements would temporarily hinder performance. The attempted remedy might easily make matters worse.

Departures from generally acceptable standards of performance sufficient to justify a demand for change can, however, be envisaged. Continued effectiveness will depend crucially upon the preservation of skills and conventions which have been built up over the years. That will depend in turn upon an ability to recruit the right calibre of staff and to maintain a reputation for independence of judgement. In the European Union, a perception that Commissioners are yielding to chauvinistic or protectionist pressures from their governments might promote a case for a more independent European competition authority. On the domestic scene, ministerial interventions on apparently partisan grounds could similarly promote a case for curbing the powers of the Secretary of State to intervene in individual cases. A perception of arrogance, bias, or bureaucratic ineptness may, on the other hand, lead to demands for more detailed accountability and day-to-day political supervision.

In most respects the prospects for institutional change are therefore uncertain. In one respect, however, change is inevitable. It will sooner or later prove necessary to regularise the present largely informal relationship between the competition authorities and the regulators of the public utilities. A spirit of give and take could, however, enable the present regime to survive for many years.

E   THE INTERNATIONAL DIMENSION

Competition policy has already come to be regarded as a means of removing barriers to international trade, and further developments in that direction may be expected. In the longer term there is a prospect of setting up an international body of rules on competition law, possibly within the framework of the World Trade Organisation. In the meantime, piecemeal developments such as the adoption of European Union regulations throughout the European Economic Association, and the establishment of the Antitrust Agreement between the Community and the United States, are likely to broaden the reach of competition policy and increase its effectiveness.

F   CONCLUSIONS

Although there are considerable uncertainties concerning future developments, they need not affect a businessman whose main concern is to know how to avoid conflict with the rules of competition policy. Evasion of those rules is likely to become more difficult and to carry much higher penalties, however.

List of Cases

Sources

All ER: All England Law Reports
Cm and Cmnd (and HC): Monopolies and Mergers Commission Reports
CMLR: Common Market Law Reports
ECLR: *European Competition Law Review*
ECR: European Court Reports
OFT: Office of Fair Trading Reports
OJ and JO: *Official Journal* of the European Union
RP: the restrictive Practices Court
US: United States Court Reports
WLR: Weekly Law Reports

References

(See Annex 4.1 for a list of official publications.)

Areeda and Turner (1975) Predatory Pricing and Related Practices under Section 2 of the Sherman Act: A Comment', *Harvard Law Review*, 697, 1975.

Baumol, W.J (1961) *Economic Theory and Operations Analysis*, Prentice-Hall, pp. 207–17.

Baumol, W.J (1982) 'Contestable Markets', *American Economic Review*, Vol. 72 No. 1, March 1982.

Baumol, W.J., J.C. Panzar, and R.D. Willig (1982) *Contestable Markets and the Theory of Industry Structure*, Harcourt Brace Jovanovich.

Bellamy, C.W. and G.D. Child (1987) *Common Market Law of Competition*, Sweet & Maxwell.

Blake, D. (1990) *Financial Market Analysis*, McGraw-Hill.

Bork, R.H. (1978) *The Antitrust Paradox: A Policy at War with Itself*, Basic Books Inc.

Borrie, Sir G. (1991) Evidence to the House of Commons Trade and Industry Committee Session 1991–2, 1st report: Takeovers & Mergers.

Carlsberg, B. (1988) *The Control of British Telecommunications Prices*, Office of Telecommunications.

Chiplin, B. and M. Wright (1987) *The Logic of Mergers*, Hobart Paper No. 107, Institute of Economic Affairs.

Comp Rep (No) (Year) *The Annual Report on Competition Policy*, The Commission of the European Union.

DGFT (Year) *The Annual Report of the Director-General of Fair Trading*, HMSO.

DTI (1978) *A Review of Monopolies and Mergers Policy. A Consultative Document*, Cmnd 7198, HMSO.

DTI (1979) *Review of Restrictive Trade Practices Policy. A Consultative Document*, Cmnd 7512 HMSO.

DTI (1988) *Mergers Policy: A Department of Trade and Industry Paper on the Policy and Procedures of Merger Control*, HMSO.

DTI (1988) *Review of Restrictive Trade Practices Policy, A Consultative Document*, Cm 331, HMSO.

DTI (1992) *Abuse of Market Power. A Consultative Document*. Cm 2100, HMSO.

Elliott, D.C and J.D. Gribbin 'The Abolition of Cartels and Structural Change in the United Kingdom' in Jaquemine and de Jong (eds) *Welfare Aspects of Industrial Markets*, Lieden.

Fairburn, J.A. and J.A. Kay (eds) (1989) *Mergers and Mergers Policy*, Oxford University Press.

Friedman, M. (1966) *Essays in Positive Economics*, Phoenix Books.

George, K. (1989) 'Do We need a Mergers Policy?' in Fairburn and Kay, op. cit.

Goyder, D.G. (1992) *EC Competition Law*, Clarendon Press.

Green, N. (1986) *Commercial Agreements and Competition Law*, Graham & Trotmam.

Holl, P. and J.F. Pickering (1986) *The Determinants and Effects of Actual, Abandoned and Contested Mergers*, UMIST mimeo (referred to in DTI 1988).

Howe, M. (1988) 'Franchising and Restrictive Practices Law', *European Competition Law Review*, Vol. 9 Issue 4.

Howe, M. (1994) *Recent Developments in United Kingdom Competition Law and Policy*, and Proceedings of the 13th Annual Anti-Trust Law Conference, Robinson College Cambridge 27–30 September 1994.

House of Commons (1995) *UK Policy on Monopolies* Session 1994–95 Trade and Industry Committee. Fifth Report. HC 249. HMSO, London.

HM Treasury (1991) *Economic Appraisal in Central Government*, HMSO London.

Little, I.D.M (1957) *A Critique of Welfare Economics*, Oxford University Press.

Littlechild, S.C. (1986) *The Fallacy of the Mixed Economy*, Hobart Paper No. 80, Institute of Economic Affairs.

Livy *The Early History of Rome*, tr. de Selincourt.

Meade, J.S. (1968) 'Is the New Industrial State Inevitable', *Economic Journal* 78, p. 372.

Morrison, S.A. and Winston, C. (1987) Empirical Implications and Tests of the Contestability Hypothesis', *Journal of Law and Economics,* Philip Allan Vol. XXX, April 1987.

Neven, D., R. Nuttall and P. Seabright (1993) *Merger in Daylight* Centre for Economic Policy Research, London.

OECD (1989) *Competition Policy and Intellectual Property Rights*. Organisation for Economic Cooperation and Development, Paris. Penguin Classics 1960.

Ravenscroft, D. and F.M. Scherer (1988) *Mergers, Sell-offs and Economic Efficiency*, Brookings Institute.

Reekie, W.D. (1979) *Industry, Prices and Markets*, Philip Allan.

Schwartz, M (1986) 'The Nature and Scope of Contestability Theory', *Oxford Economic Papers* 38, pp. 37–57.

Scherer, F.M. (1980) *Industrial Structure and Market Performance*, Rand McNally, Chicago.

Swan, D. *et al.* (1974) 'Competition in British Industry. Restrictive Practices Legislation' in *Theory and Practice*, Unwin University Books.

Van Gerven, G. and E. N. Varin (1994) 'The Woodpulp Case and the Future of Concertation Practice' *Common Market Law Review,* Vol. 31, No. 3 June 1994.

Whish, R. (1988) *Competition Law*, Butterworths 1985.

Williamson, O. (1987) *Antitrust Economics*, Blackwell.

Winch, D.M. (1971) *Analytical Welfare Economics*, Penguin.

Index